Immersed Into God Interactive Training Manual

Pouring out the Life

that Jesus Put Inside You

Andy Hayner

ISBN: 1505395976
ISBN-13: 978-1505395976

DEDICATION

To the many people who made
substantial personal investments in my life in Christ,
especially those who helped established
my foundation in Christ:

Todd Geralds and Weyman Prayter-
the men who discipled me as a new believer in college

Winston Kennedy-
the man who first took me to the mission field

John French-
the missionary who showed me how to dig into the Word of God

and

To my brothers and sisters in Christ around the world
who are making disciples of Jesus Christ!
May you continue to rejoice in the Lord ALWAYS!
Your joy in Him is contagious!

TABLE of CONTENTS

INTRODUCTION

Most believers only dream of living in the power of the fullness of Jesus Christ. God wants to "unto righteousness" and make us the answer to those dreams. We were never meant to *only* dream of walking in the fullness of Jesus Christ. God desires that each of us are discipled by those who can help us discover and activate everything that Jesus Christ put inside of us when we were born again. God wants every person *"to attain to the measure of the stature of the fullness of Christ."* (Eph. 4:13) However, His plan for us to reach this destiny is to **use us** to help one another attain to that stature. Each of us has been authorized by Jesus Christ to *"Go, make disciples"* who are *"fully trained,* **just like their Master***."*

This interactive training manual is intended to provide a tool for ordinary believers to discover and walk in the supernatural life of Jesus Christ and impact the world around them. Although this training manual is based on my book, *Immersed into God,* it covers this material in an interactive fashion that is perfect for small groups, discipleship relationships, and personal study.

Each lesson has a simple structure that facilitates personal interaction, Biblical learning, and hands-on activation. The usefulness and adaptability of this structure has been proven in the trenches of church planting movements around the world and in my own personal ministry as well.

Each meeting is divided into three sections 1) Look Back, 2) Lesson, and 3) Look Out.

The "Look Back" section gives everyone an opportunity to share highlights from the past week in two specific areas. People are encouraged to share any insights, lessons, or encouragement from what God is doing **in us** to change us more into the image of Jesus Christ. Also, everyone is asked to share a highlight from something that God has done **through us to touch others**. This keeps the focus on God (instead of ourselves) and facilitates the body of Christ connecting in a meaningful way as we pass on to others what Jesus Christ has given to us.

The "Lesson" section of the meeting is spent looking into the Word of God together. The Scripture is our teacher and the Holy Spirit is our guide as we directly interact with the Scriptures together. Every lesson is packed with Scriptures and guiding questions with specific points of observation to help you draw out life changing revelations. Together, you will have your eyes opened to the treasures of God's Word as the Spirit of God works in His people so that we are fully trained and useful for every good work.

The "Look Out" section focuses implementing the truths we have discovered *outside of our meeting time*. Each "Look Out" portion of the meeting has a time to practice, plan, and pray. You will do things like role play exercises, hands-on ministry, make plans for various personal or ministry objectives, and (of course) pray for one another.

This interactive training manual can be used in individually. However, it is designed especially for personal discipleship relationships and/or small groups to lay a solid foundation for a supernatural lifestyle of advancing the Kingdom of God. Although it can be used independently, group leaders are strongly encouraged to use this book alongside the *Immersed into God* book, which provides more detailed examples important background information that will help you be fully prepared for questions you may face for yourself or others in your group.

Each chapter is loaded with Biblical content and practical exercises, so it may be necessary to give yourselves more than one week to truly incorporate the teachings into your life. Each new lesson will activate you to walk in another aspect of living as a supernatural disciple of Jesus Christ. Each chapter also has optional video content (available through FullSpeedImpact.com) that can be used to supplement the written material.

We are called to make disciples of Jesus Christ, not ourselves. Yet God's plan is to so transform our lives that others can clearly see Jesus Christ living through us, so that we can say, "Follow me as I follow Christ." As you follow Jesus, be sure to take other people with you. I would encourage and challenge everyone who is going through this material to identify at least one other person that they can take through these same lessons. This book provides a simple tool that anyone can use to make disciples. Not only will this benefit them, it will also benefit you. The best way to learn is to teach others!

By all means, resist the comfort zone of merely becoming a Bible study. Live it out! Live out your call as an ambassador of Jesus Christ and make the nations rejoice!

Lastly, if you are leading a group that is going through this material, be sure to read Appendix 1- Suggestions for Immersed into God group leaders! Also be sure to take advantage of the additional resources I have available at my website, FullSpeedImpact.com. You'll find lots of free online video messages and other equipping resources that will help you walk in the fullness of Jesus Christ and make disciples who do the same.

God bless you!

CHAPTER 1
GOD'S LOVE- OUR MISSION AND OUR LIFE

I. LOOK BACK-

A. How have you experienced **God at work *in you*** this past week? Share a highlight, an insight from Scripture, or lesson that has encouraged you.

B. How have you experienced **God at work *through you* to touch** others this past week? How have you taken steps of faith to demonstrate the Kingdom of God to others this week? What did you experience? Share any highlights or challenges.

II. LESSON

In this lesson, we will look at God's mission for all His children. If someone were to ask you, "What is your mission in life," what would you say? Write your answer below:

THE MISSION OF A CHILD OF GOD

If we are unclear about God's mission for our lives, it will be very easy for us to get pulled off track. Since the Christian life is "*no longer me who lives, but Christ who lives in me*" one of the best ways to understand our mission is to see how Jesus Christ described His own mission.

Video 1.1 (7 min.) Introduction & Kingdom Culture Shift

Note: Supplemental training videos are available at FullSpeedImpact.com.

1) What do the passages below tell us about Jesus' mission?
a. UNDERLINE those parts of the verses below that describe Jesus's mission.
b. CIRCLE the phrases that describe the kinds of people that were the focus of Jesus' mission.

"For even the Son of Man came not to be served but to serve, and to give his life as a ransom for many." Mark 10:45

"The Spirit of the Lord is upon me, because he has anointed me to proclaim good news to the poor. He has sent me to proclaim liberty to the captives and recovering of sight to the blind, to set at liberty those who are oppressed, to proclaim the year of the Lord's favor." Luke 4:18-19

For the Son of Man came to seek and to save the lost." Luke 19:10

Go and learn what this means, "I desire Mercy, and not sacrifice." For I came not to call the righteous, but sinners" Matt. 9:13

And Jesus said to them, "Let us go on to the next towns, that I may preach there also, for that is why I came." And he went throughout all Galilee, preaching in their synagogues and casting out demons." Mark 1:38-39

Before Jesus died a redeeming death, He lived a redemptive life.

The thief comes only to steal and kill and destroy. I came that they may have life and have it abundantly. John 10:10

I glorified you on earth, having accomplished the work that you gave me to do. And now, Father, glorify me in your own presence with the glory that I had with you before the world existed. I have manifested your name to the people whom you gave me out of the world. Yours they were, and you gave them to me, and they have kept your word. John 17:4-6

Whoever makes a practice of sinning is of the devil, for the devil has been sinning from the beginning. The reason the Son of God appeared was to destroy the works of the devil. 1Jn 3:8

2) Review the verses above.
a. **SHADE** those parts of Jesus' mission that He still intends to do through believers today (in some respect).

b. Look at every place that your **UNDERLINES** (which indicate Jesus' mission) and your **SHADING** (indicating your mission) overlap. What do you learn from these overlaps about the relationship between Jesus' mission and God's mission for you?

c. What do these verses show you about God's heart towards people?

d. Think about how knowing Jesus has already impacted your lifestyle, your goals, the way you see other people. How have you already experienced "Christ in you" changing your own heart to adopt His mission for your own life?

GOD'S PROMISES TO ACCOMPLISH HIS MISSION

In order to fully participate in the promises of God that are provided for us in Christ, we must align our lives with the purpose for which gave His promises.

| Video 1.2
(5 min.)

God's Man and
God's Mission |

1) In the passages that follow,

a. **UNDERLINE** every promise of God.

b. **CIRCLE** every phrase that indicates the sort of lifestyle that is aligned with the purpose for which God gave His promise.

"But you will receive power when the Holy Spirit has come upon you, and you will be my witnesses in Jerusalem and in all Judea and Samaria, and to the end of the earth." Acts 1:8

"But seek first the Kingdom of God and his righteousness, and all these things will be added to you." Matt. 6:33

"God is able to make all grace abound to you, so that having all sufficiency in all things at all times, you may abound in every good work." 2 Cor. 9:8

"Therefore, my brothers, whom I love and long for, my joy and crown, stand firm thus in the Lord, my beloved… do not be anxious about anything, but in everything by prayer and supplication with thanksgiving let your requests be made known to God. And the peace of God, which surpasses all understanding, will guard your hearts and your minds in Christ Jesus." Phil. 4:1, 6-7

"For whoever would save his life will lose it, but whoever loses his life for my sake and the gospel's will save it." Mark 8:35

"I do all things for the sake of the gospel, that I may become a fellow partaker of it." (1 Cor. 9:23)

"He has granted to us his precious and very great promises, so that through them you may become partakers of the divine nature, having escaped from the corruption that is in the world because of sinful desire." 2 Pet. 1:4

"We know that for those who love God all things work together for good, for those who are called according to his purpose." Rom. 8:28

2) a. Based on your observations in the previous passages, how would you describe the relationship between God's promises, God's purpose, and our lifestyle?

b. Why is it important to recognize the relationship between God's promises, God's purpose, and our lifestyle?

3) a. Can you think of any examples of someone attempting to apply the promises of God while resisting the lifestyle that aligns with God's purposes?

b. What are the consequences of attempting to exercise faith in God's promises without aligning our lives to God's mission?

JESUS GIVES US OUR MISSION FROM GOD

Although God incorporates everything that makes us each one of us unique into His plan for our lives, His mission for each of us is the same. We can summarize elements that make up our mission as follows:

We REACH, PREACH, DEMONSTRATE, and DISCIPLE. In other words, we go to people and share the good news of Jesus Christ in word and deed and equip those who believe to walk in all the fullness of Jesus Christ.

1) Read the following passages of Scripture that describe our mission. As you read these passages, identify each of these elements of our mission as follows:

> Video 1.3
> (10 min.)
>
> Redemptive Relationships

- **UNDERLINE** the phrases that indicate that we are to **REACH** out to people.

- **CIRCLE** the phrases that indicate that we are to **PREACH** the gospel.

- **PUT A BOX** around the phrases that indicate that we are to **DEMONSTRATE** the reality of the Kingdom of God.

- **SHADE** those phrases that indicate that we are to **DISCIPLE** those who believe.

And Jesus came and said to them, "All authority in heaven and on earth has been given to me. Go therefore and make disciples of all nations, baptizing them in the name of the Father and of the Son and of the Holy Spirit, teaching them to observe all that I have commanded you. And behold, I am with you always, to the end of the age." Matt.28:18-20

And he said to them, "Go into all the world and proclaim the gospel to the whole creation. Whoever believes and is baptized will be saved, but whoever does not believe will be condemned. And these signs will accompany those who believe: in my name they will cast out demons; they will speak in new tongues; they will pick up serpents with their hands; and if they drink any deadly poison, it will not hurt them; they will lay their hands on the sick, and they will recover." Mark16:15-18

Then he opened their minds to understand the Scriptures, and said to them, "Thus it is written, that the Christ should suffer and on the third day rise from the dead, and that repentance and forgiveness of sins should be proclaimed in his name to all nations, beginning from Jerusalem. You are witnesses of these things. And behold, I am sending the promise of my Father upon you. But stay in the city until you are clothed with power from on high." Luke 24:45-49

> ## Living out our mission is not merely a new style of living. It's the expression of a new form of life— the divine nature of God.

"But you will receive power when the Holy Spirit has come upon you, and you will be my witnesses in Jerusalem and in all Judea and Samaria, and to the end of the earth." Acts 1:8

God chose to make known how great among the nations are the riches of the glory of this mystery, which is Christ in you, the hope of glory. Him we proclaim, warning everyone and teaching everyone with all wisdom, that we may present everyone mature in Christ. For this I toil, struggling with all his energy that he powerfully works within me. Col. 1:27-29

For we must all appear before the judgment seat of Christ, so that each one may receive what is due for what he has done in the body, whether good or evil. Therefore, knowing the fear of the Lord, we persuade others. But what we are is known to God, and I hope it is known also to your conscience For the love of Christ controls us, because we have concluded this: that one has died for all, therefore all have died; and he died for all, that those who live might no longer live for themselves but for him who for their sake died and was raised… All this is from God, who through Christ reconciled us to himself and gave us the ministry of reconciliation; that is, in Christ God was reconciling the world to himself, not counting their trespasses against them, and entrusting to us the message of reconciliation. Therefore, we are ambassadors for Christ, God making his appeal through us. 2 Cor. 5:10-20

2) Based on the preceding passages, what are some of the motivations for our mission?

The Kingdom of God is not merely the goal of our ministry. It must also be the *means* of our ministry.

---

3) a. What do these Scriptures indicate regarding any DIVINE RESOURCES God provides to us so that we can carry out our mission? List these DIVINE RESOURCES below:

b. Which of these DIVINE RESOURCES have your experienced personally?

c. Which of these DIVINE RESOURCES have you *not yet* experienced personally?

4) a. What are some ways God can use us to help one another accomplish God's mission for our lives?

b. Who do you believe God may be wanting you to help? How?

III. LOOK OUT:

PRACTICE

1. a. With a partner, practice responding to the following scenario:

You have an unbelieving friend that has learned that you are planning to go on a mission trip to Thailand. While you are sharing a cup of coffee, they ask you the following question, "Why are you going to Thailand to proselytize those people? Don't you think that's a little arrogant to push your religion on them?" Based on what you've learned about Jesus' mission and God's mission for us, practice responding to this question in 5 minutes or less. Be as persuasive and compelling as possible.

b. Switch roles and allow your partner to practice their own response.

c. Give and get feedback. What were the strong points of your response? What could make it better?

d. Repeat the role playing exercise again and incorporate the feedback you received.

PLAN

a. Where do you see a disconnect between your current lifestyle and the mission that Jesus has for you?

b. What changes are you going to make to better align your life with God's mission for you?

c. The best way for you to grow spiritually is to pass on what you are receiving from God. Who do you know that you could help (from 4 a in the lesson)? Is there someone that you know with whom you could share this lesson? Make a plan.

d. This week, read "Appendix 2- What if I don't feel led?".

e. Keep a "Mission Journal" this week. Each day make a list of the things that you did that day that connected strongly with the mission Jesus gave us. Bullet points are fine. No need to make this a literary masterpiece. This journal is for your own benefit. However, next week you will have an opportunity to share what you felt good about, where you recognized opportunities for growth, and what you learned about yourself from this exercise.

PRAY

a. Share your plan for "changes you are going to make" (#b above) and pray for one another.

b. If anyone needs healing or prayer, lay hands and minister to one another.

CHAPTER 2

THE SUPERNATURAL LIFE OF CHRIST- THE KEY TO THE CHRISTIAN LIFESTYLE

I. LOOK BACK-

A. How have you experienced God at work in you this past week? What did you learn from your "Mission Journal" assignment? What did you feel good about? What opportunities from growth did you recognize? Share any highlights, lessons, insights or encouragement.

B. How have you experienced God at work *through you* to touch others this past week? How have you taken steps of faith to demonstrate the Kingdom to others this week? What happened? Share any highlights or challenges.

II. LESSON

There is an unbreakable connection between living in the power of God's Spirit and living in God's mission. The key to fulfilling God's mission is partaking of God's divine nature in Christ. God wants our lifestyle to be an overflow of His redeeming love.

> **Video 2.1**
> **(5 min.)**
>
> **Living the Life Jesus Put Inside You**

What are some of the effects of people attempting to fulfill God's mission in their own way by their own power instead of becoming an overflowing container of God's own Spirit?

THE SOURCE OF JESUS' LIFE

Jesus said that "a disciple who is fully trained will be just like His master." Jesus made it clear that while He lived on earth, His humanity was hosting and expressing a higher form of life- divine life! Although Jesus lived as a man, He lived by His Father's divine life. In the process, Jesus shows us how born again children of God partake of the divine nature.

1) As you read the following Scriptures:
a. UNDERLINE each time Jesus indicates He can't live the life He is living by His own human resources.

b. CIRCLE the phrases in which Jesus indicates how He, as a man, is able to live by His Father's divine life.

So Jesus said to them, "Truly, truly, I say to you, the Son can do nothing of his own accord, but only what he sees the Father doing. For whatever the Father does, that the Son does likewise. For the Father loves the Son and shows him all that he himself is doing. And greater works than these will he show him, so that you may marvel. John 5:19-20

Human beings were created to contain God.
We are God's image bearers.

"I can do nothing on my own. As I hear, I judge, and my judgment is just, because I seek not my own will but the will of him who sent me. Joh 5:30

So Jesus said to them, "When you have lifted up the Son of Man, then you will know that I am he, and that I do nothing on my own authority, but speak just as the Father taught me. And he who sent me is with me. He has not left me alone, for I always do the things that are pleasing to him." John 8:28-29

If you had known me, you would have known my Father also. From now on you do know him and have seen him." Philip said to him, "Lord, show us the Father, and it is enough for us." Jesus said to him, "Have I been with you so long, and you still do not know me, Philip? Whoever has seen me has seen the Father. How can you say, 'Show us the Father'? Do you not believe that I am in the Father and the Father is in me? The words that I say to you I do not speak on my own authority, but the Father who dwells in me does his works. Believe me that I am in the Father and the Father is in me, or else believe on account of the works themselves. John 14:7-14

Jesus only did what He saw His Father doing. How does this passage show us how we see the Father?

What are some things we see the Father doing in Christ?

2. In the following passages:
a. UNDERLINE each time the Word of God indicates that you can't live the life God wants without participating in God's divine life.

b. CIRCLE the phrases that indicate *how* you, as a born again human, are able to live by God's divine life today.

c. ANSWER any questions by referring the passage of Scripture directly preceding the question.

Yet a little while and the world will see me no more, but you will see me. Because I live, you also will live. In that day you will know that I am in my Father, and you in me, and I in you. John 14:19-20

Why do we have to wait for the indwelling of the Holy Spirit to know that Jesus is in the Father, and we are in Him, and He is in us? What kind of knowledge is Jesus talking about?

Abide in me, and I in you. As the branch cannot bear fruit by itself, unless it abides in the vine, neither can you, unless you abide in me. I am the vine; you are the branches. Whoever abides in me and I in him, he it is that bears much fruit, for apart from me you can do nothing…If you abide in me, and my words abide in you, ask whatever you wish, and it will be done for you. By this my Father is glorified, that you bear much fruit and so prove to be my disciples. John 15:4-8

How does God feel about bearing much fruit in you? Why is it important to understand that?

If we want to bear much fruit, what should we be focused on- fruit bearing, or living in Christ? Why?

Is it possible for someone live in union with Christ without bearing fruit?

And this is eternal life, that they know you the only true God, and Jesus Christ whom you have sent. John 17:3

Can a believer experience eternal life now? How?

For through the law I died to the law, so that I might live to God. I have been crucified with Christ. It is no longer I who live, but Christ who lives in me. And the life I now live in the flesh I live by the faith of the Son of God, who loved me and gave himself for me. I do not nullify the grace of God, for if righteousness were through the law, then Christ died for no purpose. Gal. 2:19-21

Describe the relationship that dead people and the Law of Moses have with one another. How many Laws did God give to regulate the conduct of dead people?

Does God intend for our conduct to be regulated by the Laws of Moses, or by the new nature He has given to us? (see also, 1 Tim. 1:8-11)

If a Christian is dead to the Law — according to Gal. 2:19-20, what governs the conduct of a believer?

Is the resurrected Lord Jesus Christ in heaven trying to live up to the Laws of Moses, or is He simply living unto God? What does this say about how Christ lives IN US today?

Would "Christ living in you" ever condone sin? How difficult is it for Jesus Christ to live in victory over sin?

But when the fullness of time had come, God sent forth his Son, born of woman, born under the law, to redeem those who were under the law, so that we might receive adoption as sons. And because you are sons, God has sent the Spirit of his Son into our hearts, crying, "Abba! Father!" Gal. 4:4-7

What is the Spirit of the Son doing? Where?

What does this show us about how we can tap into His life in us?

May grace and peace be multiplied to you in the knowledge of God and of Jesus our Lord. His divine power has granted to us all things that pertain to life and godliness, through the knowledge of him who called us to his own glory and excellence, by which he has granted to us his precious and very great promises, so that through them you may become partakers of the divine nature, having escaped from the corruption that is in the world because of sinful desire. 2 Pet. 1:2-4

According to this passage, do Christians grow spiritually by 1) getting God to give us more, or 2) learning to walk in the fullness of all He has already given us?

What difference does this make?

God not only declares us to be righteous, but also makes us righteous by placing His own Spirit within us.

That which was from the beginning, which we have heard, which we have seen with our eyes, which we looked upon and have touched with our hands, concerning the word of life—the life was made manifest, and we have seen it, and testify to it and proclaim to you the eternal life, which was with the Father and was made manifest to us—that which we have seen and heard we proclaim also to you, so that you too may have fellowship with us; and indeed our fellowship is with the Father and with his Son Jesus Christ. And we are writing these things so that our joy may be complete. 1 John 1:1-4

When will believers be able to experience fellowship with the Father and Son?

In what way does sharing Jesus Christ with others make our joy complete?

3) SUMMARIZE: How would you describe the similarities between the way in which Jesus lived by His Father's life and how we are to live our lives today?

PUTTING ON YOUR "JESUS SUIT"

The good news is that through Jesus Christ God has given us the same relationship with Him as Jesus Christ. We get to "put on Christ" before the Father and go to God as a son, in the Son.

1) In each of the following passages of Scripture
a. CIRCLE those phrases that indicate *how* we come to the Father wearing our "Jesus suit"
b. UNDERLINE those phrases that indicate the benefits of wearing our "Jesus suit"

Jesus said, "I am the door. If anyone enters by me, he will be saved and will go in and out and find pasture." John 10:9

Jesus said to him, "I am the way, and the truth, and the life. No one comes to the Father except through me. If you had known me, you would have known my Father also. From now on you do know him and have seen him." John14:6-7

Abide in me, and I in you. As the branch cannot bear fruit by itself, unless it abides in the vine, neither can you, unless you abide in me. I am the vine; you are the branches. Whoever abides in me and I in him, he it is that bears much fruit, for apart from me you can do nothing. John 15:4-5

Therefore, since we have been justified by faith, we have peace with God through our Lord Jesus Christ. Through him we have also obtained access by faith into this grace in which we stand, and we rejoice in hope of the glory of God. Rom. 5:1-2

But God, being rich in mercy, because of the great love with which he loved us, even when we were dead in our trespasses, made us alive together with Christ—by grace you have been saved—and raised us up with him and seated us with him in the heavenly places in Christ Jesus, so that in the coming ages he might show the immeasurable riches of his grace in kindness toward us in Christ Jesus. Eph 2:4-7

God is faithful, by whom you were called into the fellowship of his Son, Jesus Christ our Lord. 1 Cor. 1:9

For through him we both have access in one Spirit to the Father. Eph. 2:18

So you also must consider yourselves dead to sin and alive to God in Christ Jesus…Do not present your members to sin as instruments for unrighteousness, but present yourselves to God as those who have been brought from death to life, and your members to God as instruments for righteousness. Rom. 6:11-13

This was according to the eternal purpose that he has realized in Christ Jesus our Lord, in whom we have boldness and access with confidence through our faith in him. Eph. 3:11-12

As you received Christ Jesus the Lord, so walk in him, rooted and built up in him and established in the faith, just as you were taught, abounding in thanksgiving. Col. 2:6-7

1) In your own words, describe how the Father feels about Jesus Christ? Why does He feel this way?

2) In your own words, describe how it feels to realize that God has chosen to adopt you into the same place in His heart and give you the relationship He has with Jesus Christ as your relationship with Him?

3) What is the difference between merely presenting yourself to God, and presenting yourself to God as those who are alive from the dead, seated with Christ in heavenly places?

III. LOOK OUT

PRACTICE

1) **Declarations-** Use the Scriptures listed under "Putting on Your Jesus Suit" to turn them into prayer and declarations of faith. One person will lead, the others will repeat what the leader says. Use the Scriptures as a launching pad and let your heart soar into the embrace of the Father!

For example, John 10:9-Jesus said, "I am the door. If anyone enters by me, he will be saved and will go in and out and find pasture." John 10:9

Leader: Father I enter your presence (group repeats) By entering into Jesus Christ (group repeats) He is my door (group repeats) I step into Him and enter into Your presence (group repeats) I am inside of Jesus Christ and I am saved (group repeats) I am wearing His righteousness (group repeats) He wore my sins (group repeats) I am inside of Jesus Christ and He is inside of Me (group repeats) I find nourishment for my soul in the Father's presence (group repeats).

2) **Role Play-**
a. **With a partner, practice responding to the following scenario:**

You have friend who is a sincere believer in Jesus Christ. However, they have been raised in a very strict, often legalistic church environment. They struggle with a constant fear of rejection and feelings like God is disappointed with them. They ask you over for coffee to seek your encouragement. How can you use your understanding of our union with God in Christ to help them begin to enjoy fellowship with God? You have five minutes.

b. Switch roles and allow your partner to practice their own response.

c. Give and get feedback. What were the strong points of your response? What could make it better?

d. Repeat the role playing exercise again and incorporate the feedback you received.

3) Acknowledge Your Inheritance in Christ:

a. As a group, list as many "spiritual blessings" as you can think of. Write them down as people brainstorm the blessings they remember.

b. **DECLARATIONS:** With your list in front of you, as a group, take time to declare that these blessings are yours in Christ and to thank God.

"In Christ, I have been blessed with…" etc.

PLAN

1. Are you aware of any ways that your mindsets and lifestyle doesn't "fit" your new divine nature? What adjustments are you aware of that you need to make in order to make room for more "divine LIFE"?

2. a. Every day for the next month (and the rest of your life), set aside some time speak to God from inside of Jesus Christ. Enjoy the relationship that Father has with Jesus Christ as YOUR relationship. Dedicate this time without speaking to God about any of your needs, failures, or things you want His help with. Simply be with God and enjoy the Father's relationship with the Son as your relationship. Spend enough time to allow your soul to "absorb" this perspective. Use the Scriptures

related to life in Christ as a spring board for these times. Ephesians 1, Romans 6, or Psalm 23 are easy places to start. [1]

b. Stop letting guilt, worry, and shame hold you back from the living in the Father's embrace. Stop chasing your satisfaction and security in the stuff you have and eyes of other people. Let the Love of God fill you. Let it control you!

c. Never stop doing 2a and 2b.

3. PRAY

a. Share your plan for "changes you are going to make" (#2a page 15) and pray for one another.

b. If anyone needs healing or prayer, lay hands and minister to one another.

---

[1] I have written *Spirit Cry- Declarations of a Child of God in the Embrace of the Father* as a devotional tool to help believers establish the practice of speaking and hearing from the Spirit of the Son of God in your heart by using God's Word. It is a unique and very powerful tool that can be very helpful to build this practice into your life.

CHAPTER 3
LET'S GET WITH IT

I. LOOK BACK-

A. How have you experienced **God at work** *in you* this past week? What did you experience as you made time to meet with God in your "Jesus suit" this week? Share any highlights, lessons, insights or encouragement.

B. How have you experienced **God at work** *through you* to touch others this past week? How have you taken steps of faith to demonstrate the Kingdom to others this week? What happened? Share any highlights or challenges.

II. LESSON

We have been created by a God who is perfect love. We have been created to participate in and manifest the love that flows between the Father and the Son in the Holy Spirit. The Father dwells inside the Son by the Holy Spirit. The Son dwells inside the Father by the Holy Spirit. Through Jesus Christ, we have been brought into this eternal exchange of love.

God's method of ministry is to send a person filled with Himself.

In this lesson we will look at God's way of ministry — people saturated with Himself making disciples through redemptive relationships.

GOD WITH US... ON THE INSIDE!

God does more than send us a book or tell us what He wants us to do. He is "God with us". He moves into our lives to empower us with His presence.

> **Video 3.1**
> **(10 min.)**
>
> **Get WITH it**

1) In the following Scriptures,
a. UNDERLINE the phrases that indicate the importance of "being *with*" God in order to become an overflowing container of His Spirit.

b. CIRCLE the phrases that indicate *God's way* of relating to people.

c. ANSWER any questions based on the verses directly preceding the question.

In the beginning was the Word, and the Word was with God, and the Word was God. He was in the beginning with God... For from his fullness we have all received, grace upon grace. For the law was given through Moses; grace and truth came through Jesus Christ. No one has ever seen God; the only God, who is at the Father's side, he has made him known. John 1:1-2, 16-18

What filled Jesus Christ?

Where did He get filled?

But Jesus answered them, "My Father is working until now, and I am working." John 5:17

And he appointed twelve (whom he also named apostles) so that they might be with him and he might send them out to preach and have authority to cast out demons. Mark 3:14-15

Why couldn't Jesus just give the apostles some books to read to prepare them ministry?

So Jesus said to them, "Truly, truly, I say to you, the Son can do nothing of his own accord, but only what he sees the Father doing. For whatever the Father does, that the Son does likewise. For the Father loves the Son and shows him all that he himself is doing. And greater works than these will he show him, so that you may marvel. John 5:19-20

How did Jesus believe the Father felt about Him?

What did this awareness produce in the life of Jesus Christ?

And if I go and prepare a place for you, I will come again and will take you to myself, that where I am you may be also... Do you not believe that I am in the Father and the Father is in me? John 14:3,10

Where was Jesus dwelling?

Where does He bring us to dwell?

An argument arose among them as to which of them was the greatest. But Jesus, knowing the reasoning of their hearts, took a child and put him by his side and said to them, "Whoever receives this child in my name receives me, and whoever receives me receives him who sent me. For he who is least among you all is the one who is great." Luke 9:46-48

I speak of what I have seen with my Father, and you do what you have heard from your father." John 8:38

During supper, when the devil had already put it into the heart of Judas Iscariot, Simon's son, to betray him, Jesus, knowing that the Father had given all things into his hands, and that he had come from God and was going back to God, rose from supper. He laid aside his outer garments, and taking a towel, tied it around his waist. Then he poured water into a basin and began to wash the disciples' feet and to wipe them with the towel that was wrapped around him. John 13:2-5

1) How would you describe the way that Jesus treated people and carried out His ministry? Where did Jesus Christ learn to treat people?

2) a. Compare and contrast the way that Jesus treats people and carried out His ministry with the way you treat people and conduct your own ministry. How is it similar? How is it dissimilar?

b. What would Jesus change about the way you relate to people and carry out your ministry if He moved into your skin? Don't guess. Ask Him.

LONE RANGER C.E.O.s or TEAMS OF DISCIPLES?

The Spirit of God is not an "independent spirit", nor is He a "control freak." The Holy Spirit connects us to God and to one another through Jesus Christ. While many are trying to use God to build and run an organization, God is seeking to build people into the image of Jesus Christ through disciple-makers filled with Himself. God doesn't treat people as resources for His vision. We ARE His vision.

2) In the following passages of Scripture,
a. UNDERLINE the phrases that show that God works through people filled with His heart.

b. CIRCLE the phrases that indicate the impact that godly people makes on the lives of others.

And He who sent Me is with Me. He has not left Me alone, for I always do the things that are pleasing to Him."… Jesus said to them again, "Peace be with you. As the Father has sent me, even so I am sending you." John 8:29 and 20:21

According to these verses, what did Jesus mean when He said "As the Father sent Me"? How did the Father send Jesus?

We were gentle among you, like a nursing mother taking care of her own children. So, being affectionately desirous of you, we were ready to share with you not only the gospel of God but also our own selves, because you had become very dear to us…For you know how, like a father with his children, we exhorted each one of you and encouraged you and charged you to walk in a manner worthy of God, who calls you into his own kingdom and glory. 1Th 2:8-12

Do you see God's heart in Paul? How?

I do not write these things to make you ashamed, but to admonish you as my beloved children. For though you have countless guides in Christ, you do not have many fathers. For I became your father in Christ Jesus through the gospel. I urge you, then, be imitators of me. That is why I sent you Timothy, my beloved and faithful child in the Lord, to remind you of my ways in Christ, as I teach them everywhere in every church. 1Co 4:14-17

Likewise you also should be glad and rejoice with me. I hope in the Lord Jesus to send Timothy to you soon, so that I too may be cheered by news of you. For I have no one like him, who will be genuinely concerned for your welfare. For they all seek their own interests, not those of Jesus Christ. But you know Timothy's proven worth, how as a son with a father he has served with me in the gospel. I hope therefore to send him just as soon as I see how it will go with me,
Phil. 2:18-23

Why did Paul feel it was necessary to send Timothy, not just a letter with his teaching? What does this show us about the importance of godly examples in our Christian growth?

The finest sermons, prettiest buildings, and best run programs in all of Christendom will never substitute for disciple-makers spending time with believers to equip them to walk in the fullness of Jesus Christ.

But thanks be to God, who put into the heart of Titus the same earnest care I have for you. For he not only accepted our appeal, but being himself very earnest he is going to you of his own accord. With him we are sending the brother who is famous among all the churches for his preaching of the gospel. 2Co 8:16-18

I am reminded of your sincere faith, a faith that dwelt first in your grandmother Lois and your mother Eunice and now, I am sure, dwells in you as well. For this reason I remind you to fan into flame the gift of God, which is in you through the laying on of my hands…You then, my child, be strengthened by the grace that is in Christ Jesus, and what you have heard from me in the presence of many witnesses entrust to faithful men who will be able to teach others also.
2Ti 1:2-6 and 2:1-2

Trace the chain of godly influence, starting with Timothy's grandmother through "others also":

Rather, speaking the truth in love, we are to grow up in every way into him who is the head, into Christ, from whom the whole body, joined and held together by every joint with which it is equipped, when each part is working properly, makes the body grow so that it builds itself up in love.
Eph 4:15-16

Therefore, if anyone cleanses himself from what is dishonorable, he will be a vessel for honorable use, set apart as holy, useful to the master of the house, ready for every good work. So flee youthful passions and pursue righteousness, faith, love, and peace, along with those who call on the Lord from a pure heart. 2Ti 2:21-22

Based on the verses above, what should our closest relationships in the body of Christ look like?

1) How have you seen Jesus Christ through His people? How has that impacted your life?

2) If God could fill your heart with His own heart for people, what would change inside of you? How would this change your lifestyle? Don't guess. Ask Him.

III. LOOK OUT:

PRACTICE

1. GROUP EXERCISE- Practice seeing Jesus Christ in one another and building one another up in Christ. As a group, share with one another, "This is how I see Jesus Christ in you" and "This is how I can see Jesus using you to advance His Kingdom" and "This is how I see Jesus at work in your life."

2. WITH the TWOs and THREEs- It's time to learn to interact with one another in a way that only Jesus Christ makes possible. Break up into groups of twos or threes.

Discuss the following questions:

➢ What is your greatest challenge in your personal walk with Christ right now?

➢ What is your greatest challenge in your ministry for the Kingdom right now?

> ➤ Then pray for one another and share any encouragement the Lord gives you.

PLAN

1. This week, take some time encourage the people who have made a difference in your life for the sake of the Kingdom. Who can you encourage? How will you express your gratitude?

2. Who could you invest some time to encourage and build them up for the sake of the Kingdom? Jot down a plan and make it happen.

3. Who do you know that is strong in areas that are a challenge for you right now? Make a plan to get together and ask them to help you get stronger in the Lord in those areas.

PRAY

If anyone needs healing or prayer, lay hands and minister to one another.

CHAPTER 4
IMMERSED INTO GOD (PART 1)

I. LOOK BACK

A. How have you experienced **God at work *in you*** this past week? Share any highlights, lessons, insights from the Word or encouragement.

B. How have you experienced **God at work *through you*** to touch others this past week? How have you taken steps of faith to demonstrate the Kingdom of God to others this week? What did you experience? Share any highlights or challenges.

II. LESSON

God wants you to be saturated with Him. If you are going to immerse yourself in God, you've got to detox from the world. It's impossible to saturate ourselves with the world and live in the power of the Holy Spirit. If we are going to cultivate a lifestyle of loving God and living in the awareness of His presence, every believer needs to spend time communing with God alone.

> ## If Jesus Christ needed to make time to be alone with God,
> ## we must make this a high priority for ourselves also.

In the Scriptures below:
a. UNDERLINE phrases that indicate HOW, WHEN, or WHERE we can spend time alone with God.

b. CIRCLE the benefits and results of cultivating a life with God in secret.

And rising very early in the morning, while it was still dark, he departed and went out to a desolate place, and there he prayed. Mar 1:35

Immediately he made his disciples get into the boat and go before him to the other side, to Bethsaida, while he dismissed the crowd. And after he had taken leave of them, he went up on the mountain to pray. Mar 6:45-46

One thing have I asked of the LORD, that will I seek after: that I may dwell in the house of the LORD all the days of my life, to gaze upon the beauty of the LORD and to inquire in his temple. For he will hide me in his shelter in the day of trouble; he will conceal me under the cover of his tent; he will lift me high upon a rock. Psalm 27:4-5

But when you pray, go into your room and shut the door and pray to your Father who is in secret. And your Father who sees in secret will reward you. Mat 6:6

My soul yearns for you in the night; my spirit within me earnestly seeks you. For when your judgments are in the earth, the inhabitants of the world learn righteousness. Isa 26:9

O LORD, in the morning you hear my voice; in the morning I prepare a sacrifice for you and watch. Psalm 5:3

Blessed is the man who walks not in the counsel of the wicked, nor stands in the way of sinners, nor sits in the seat of scoffers; but his delight is in the law of the LORD, and on his law he meditates day and night. He is like a tree planted by streams of water that yields its fruit in its season, and its leaf does not wither. In all that he does, he prospers. Psalm 1:1-3

SATURATION EVALUATION

What are you saturating yourself with? List the media influences that you partake of regularly, including books, radio, television, internet, social media, etc.

CIRCLE those things that are good, wholesome, and godly influences that are building up your faith.

SHADE those media influences that are dragging your spirit down with negativity or ungodly influences.

As you evaluate what you are saturating yourself, are there any changes you can make that will benefit you spiritually?

ENCOUNTERING JESUS CHRIST IN THE SCRIPTURES

One of the most valuable tools God has given us to establish a lifestyle of communion with Him is the Scriptures. Many times new believers turn to the Scriptures to find an answer to their problems, a promise relating to a specific need, or "chicken soup for their soul." They may turn to the Scriptures to solve a theological debate and prove their point of

> **Video 4.1**
> **(10 min.)**
>
> **Enjoying the Fellowship of Jesus Christ**

view, or to develop their list of do's and don'ts. While there may be some validity to each of these, I'd like to suggest that **none of these** are the primary reason that God has given us His Word.

A Lesson from Jesus about how to use the Scriptures

You search the Scriptures because you think that in them you have eternal life; and it is they that **bear witness about me**, *yet you refuse to* **come to me** *that* **you may have life**." John 5:39-40

The Scriptures:

- Bear witness of Jesus Christ- (who He is, His character, what He has accomplished, etc.)

- So that we can come to Him and Encounter Him personally, and

- Receive the Life that is in Him as our Life as we surrender to His Spirit

In other words, we should use the Scriptures to fellowship with God and be transformed into His likeness as we receive Him as our life.

LEARNING TO SEE, SAVOR, and SURRENDER

Here are a few keys from the Scriptures that will help get you started in your journey of discovering the depths of Jesus Christ in the Word of God:

Wherever we see God's wisdom, righteousness, sanctification or redemption, we are seeing Jesus Christ.

> *And because of him you are in Christ Jesus, who became to us* **wisdom from God, righteousness and sanctification and redemption**... 1 Cor. 1:30

Every standard or example of Christian living is a revelation of Jesus Christ.

> *I am the vine; you are the branches. Whoever abides in me and I in him, he it is that bears much fruit, for* **apart from me you can do nothing**. John 15:5

> *I have been crucified with Christ.* **It is no longer I who live, but Christ who lives in me**. *And the life I now live in the flesh I live by the faith of the Son of God, who loved me and gave himself for me.* Gal 2:20

In the Scriptures below:

a. UNDERLINE every phrase that indicates **God's wisdom, sanctification, or redemption.**

b. CIRCLE every phrase that indicates an example or standard of Christian living.

c. In the space under each verse, **write how you can SEE Jesus** as one who embodied the reality of this verse.

Example:

Trust in the LORD with all your heart, and do not lean on your own understanding.
In all your ways acknowledge him, and he will make straight your paths. Prov. 3:5-6

Jesus, you are the Spirit of Faith. You are wholehearted in your confidence in the Father. You never leaned on your own understanding. You demonstrated the knowledge of God in all You ways. You are the very way of the Father.

Count it all joy, my brothers, when you meet trials of various kinds, for you know that the testing of your faith produces steadfastness. James 1:3

Know this, my beloved brothers: let every person be quick to hear, slow to speak, slow to anger; James 1:19

If anyone thinks he is religious and does not bridle his tongue but deceives his heart, this person's religion is worthless. Religion that is pure and undefiled before God, the Father, is this: to visit orphans and widows in their affliction, and to keep oneself unstained from the world. James1:26-27

Now at Lystra there was a man sitting who could not use his feet. He was crippled from birth and had never walked. He listened to Paul speaking. And Paul, looking intently at him and seeing that he had faith to be made well, said in a loud voice, "Stand upright on your feet." And he sprang up and began walking. Acts 14:8-10

But whatever gain I had, I counted as loss for the sake of Christ. Indeed, I count everything as loss because of the surpassing worth of knowing Christ Jesus my Lord. For his sake I have suffered the loss of all things and count them as rubbish, in order that I may gain Christ Phil. 3:7-8

SAVOR and SURRENDER

In addition to using the Scriptures to SEE Jesus Christ AS the Christian life, you will need to develop the habit of coming to Him, encountering Him, fellowshipping with Him personally, heart to heart, spirit to spirit.

As we behold Jesus Christ and the glory that is in Him, by faith we simply recognize that He lives inside of us and receive His life as our own life. We surrender to His Spirit and put off anything inside of us that is not the life of Jesus Christ.

In the Scriptures below:

a. UNDERLINE every phrase that indicates that we can EXPERIENCE God because of our union with Jesus Christ

b. CIRCLE every phrase that indicates the results or benefits of experiencing God.

Oh, taste and see that the LORD is good! Blessed is the man who takes refuge in him! Psalm 34:8

Now the Lord is the Spirit, and where the Spirit of the Lord is, there is freedom. And we all, with unveiled face, beholding the glory of the Lord, are being transformed into the same image from one degree of glory to another. For this comes from the Lord who is the Spirit. 2 Cor. 3:17-18

Because you are sons, God has sent the Spirit of his Son into our hearts, crying, "Abba! Father!" Gal 4:5-6

I am the door. If anyone enters by me, he will be saved and will go in and out and find pasture. Joh 10:9

I will not leave you as orphans; I will come to you. Yet a little while and the world will see me no more, but you will see me. Because I live, you also will live. In that day you will know that I am in my Father, and you in me, and I in you. Whoever has my commandments and keeps them, he it is who loves me. And he who loves me will be loved by my Father, and I will love him and manifest myself to him." Judas (not Iscariot) said to him, "Lord, how is it that you will manifest yourself to us, and not to the world?" Jesus answered him, "If anyone loves me, he will keep my word, and my Father will love him, and we will come to him and make our home with him. John. 14:18-23

III. LOOK OUT
PRACTICE
1. Break into groups of 3 or 4 for a time to practice fellowshipping with the Lord from the Scriptures. Turn to Psalm 15 and read it out loud.

- Briefly share together, "How do you SEE Jesus Christ as the one who embodies this Scripture?" You don't need to make this a big discussion. Share just enough to make sure that no one is lost and that each person SEEs Jesus Christ in the Scripture.

- As a group, enjoy a time of SAVORING JESUS CHRIST and SURRENDERING TO HIS SPIRIT using this Scripture.
  1. Take turns leading out by reading a verse or two (just enough to SEE a little more of Jesus). Open up in praise, adoration, and expressions of faith, love and hope in Jesus Christ prompted by what you see in this verse. Allow your heart to soar as the Spirit of God brings more to mind.

  2. No "prayer-a-thons". Keep it simple. Keep it real. Keep it moving.

  3. Before moving from the verse, SURRENDER to His Spirit and put off anything that is not the life of Christ within you.

b. ROLE PLAY
You will practice explaining to someone else how to SEE, SAVOR, and SURRENDER to Jesus Christ in the Scriptures.

Here is the scenario. Your friend confides in you that they have stopped reading the Bible for themselves because they were never able to get anything meaningful out of their reading and often ended up feeling condemned by what they read. Practice sharing what you've learned in this lesson to help them.

PLAN

a. Who do you know that is a believer in Jesus Christ that you can share how to fellowship with God by SEEING, SAVORING, and SURRENDERING to Jesus Christ? Make a plan to share this lesson with them this week. Write their name(s) in the space below.

b. What is your plan to have a regular time alone with God? When? Where? How long? What changes do you need to make to protect this time? Write your plan below and share it with your group. If you have any challenges, share this with your group for prayer and counsel.

c. For those who would like additional insight and help in SEEING, SAVORING, and SURRENDERING to Jesus Christ, check out my book *SPIRIT CRY- Declarations of a Child of God in the Embrace of the Father* (available at my website FullSpeedImpact.com).

PRAY

a. Pray for one another. Ask God to make you a people of continual fellowship with Him and awareness of His presence.

b. If anyone needs healing or prayer, lay hands and minister to one another.

CHAPTER 5
SHARING YOUR JESUS STORIES
PART 1

I. LOOK BACK-

A. How have you experienced God at work in you this past week? How are you doing developing a lifestyle of enjoying time alone with God? Share any highlights, lessons, insights or encouragement that came from your time alone with God.

B. How have you experienced **God at work** ***through you*** to touch others this past week? How have you taken steps of faith to demonstrate the Kingdom of God to others this week? What did you experience? Share any highlights or challenges.

II. LESSON

You are an expert witness on how Jesus Christ makes a difference in your life. Every time you share your testimonies of God's work, the Holy Spirit is released to create faith and accomplish the same supernatural works in the lives of others.

In this lesson, you will be equipped to share several kinds of Jesus stories so that you will be able to speak to people about Jesus Christ in a way that is relevant and powerful.

THE POWER OF TESTIMONIES

1) In the following Scriptures,
a. UNDERLINE who shares the testimony and the subject of the testimony
b. CIRCLE who hears the testimony
c. SHADE the impact or result of the testimony

The man from whom the demons had gone begged that he might be with him, but Jesus sent him away, saying, "Return to your home, and declare how much God has done for you." And he went away, proclaiming throughout the whole city how much Jesus had done for him. Luke 8:38-39

And all the assembly fell silent, and they listened to Barnabas and Paul as they related what signs and wonders God had done through them among the Gentiles. Act 15:12

After greeting them, he related one by one the things that God had done among the Gentiles through his ministry. And when they heard it, they glorified God. Acts 21:19-20

So when Peter went up to Jerusalem, the circumcision party criticized him, saying, "You went to uncircumcised men and ate with them." But Peter began and explained it to them in order: "I was in the city of Joppa praying, and in a trance I saw a vision, something like a great sheet descending, being let down from heaven by its four corners, and it came down... Act 11:2-5

We want you to know, brothers, about the grace of God that has been given among the churches of Macedonia, for in a severe test of affliction, their abundance of joy and their extreme poverty have overflowed in a wealth of generosity on their part. For they gave according to their means, as I can testify, and beyond their means, of their own accord, begging us earnestly for the favor of taking part in the relief of the saints— 2 Cor.8:1-4

For not only has the word of the Lord sounded forth from you in Macedonia and Achaia, but your faith in God has gone forth everywhere, so that we need not say anything. For they themselves report concerning us the kind of reception we had among you, and how you turned to God from idols to serve the living and true God, 1 Thes.1:8-9

So the woman left her water jar and went away into town and said to the people, "Come, and see a man who told me all that I ever did. Can this be the Christ?" They went out of town and were coming to him. John 4:28-30

For we cannot but speak of what we have seen and heard. Act 4:20

And I heard a loud voice in heaven, saying, "Now the salvation and the power and the kingdom of our God and the authority of his Christ have come, for the accuser of our brothers has been thrown down, who accuses them day and night before our God." And they have conquered him by the blood of the Lamb and by the word of their testimony, for they loved not their lives even unto death. Rev. 12:10-11

Let the redeemed of the LORD say so, whom he has redeemed from trouble. For he shatters the doors of bronze and cuts in two the bars of iron. Some were fools through their sinful ways, and because of their iniquities suffered affliction; they loathed any kind of food, and they drew near to the gates of death. Then they cried to the LORD in their trouble, and he delivered them from their distress. He sent out his word and healed them, and delivered them from their destruction. Let them thank the LORD for his steadfast love, for his wondrous works to the children of man! And let them offer sacrifices of thanksgiving, and tell of his deeds in songs of joy! Psalm107:2,16-22

Then I fell down at his (the angels) feet to worship him, but he said to me, "You must not do that! I am a fellow servant with you (the apostle John) and your brothers who hold to the testimony of Jesus. Worship God." For the testimony of Jesus is the spirit of prophecy. Rev. 19:10

1) Based on the preceding Scriptures and your personal experience, what are some of the things that makes a personal testimony so powerful?

2) Based on the preceding Scriptures and your own personal experience, what are some of the situations in which it may be more effective to use a personal testimony instead of a lesson straight from the Bible (for example)? Why?

BULLET TESIMONIES

One of the easiest ways to share a testimony is what I call "Bullet Testimonies." These are sound bites or "elevator speeches." These are like captions under a picture, not the picture itself. You don't go into that much detail. They are usually just a few short sentences that convey the impact of a story without telling a story.

Here are some examples of "Bullet Testimonies":

- *"I went to church my whole life but I was the biggest hypocrite that ever lived until I really met Jesus."*

- *"I was addicted to every drug known to mankind, an atheist that hated God and hated Christians. Then God broke into my life and I've never been the same."*

- *"I used to think that every religion was the same, and I frankly still do. I can't stand religion. Religious people are the ones who killed Jesus. But Jesus is different. He's not a religion at all. He's able to give you a real relationship with God like no one else."*

- *"I was a Muslim who was contemplating being a suicide bomber so I could go to paradise. Then I learned that Jesus died for me, and it's made all the difference in my life."*

- *"I had a great career and a terrible marriage. I was heading for a divorce when I cried out to God, not even expecting an answer. Then He came crashing into my life, saved my marriage, brought balance, and put everything in perspective. He'll do the same thing for you too. I know it."*

- *"I didn't want anything to do with Jesus, because I didn't want Him to be real. I wanted to do my own thing... until my own thing destroyed two marriages and landed me in jail. Then I hoped Jesus might be real. But ever since I called out to Him and asked Him to save me, I **know** He's real."*

BULLET TESTIMONY EXERCISE:

Use this space to write a few notes for your own "Bullet Stories".

SALVATION STORIES

One of the most basic Jesus stories you need to learn to share is your salvation story. As you begin to develop your story, you should picture someone you know who isn't yet a believer in Jesus Christ. You are going to be sharing this story with them. You're not writing a book or preparing a sermon. You are not sharing your life's story or every sordid detail. You're preparing yourself to share a brief story as part of a conversation with a friend to explain the difference that knowing Jesus Christ has made in your life.

> **Video 5.1**
> **(12 min.)**
>
> **Sharing Your**
> **Salvation Story**

There are three major sections that you'll have in your story:

1. **BEFORE/WITHOUT:** What is your life like before or without the LIFE in Jesus Christ?
2. **REALIZATION/CONVERSION:** How did you come to understand what Jesus did for you and first become a follower of Jesus Christ?
3. **DIFFERENCE/CHANGE:** What difference does Jesus Christ make in your life?

Here are a few pointers to keep in mind as you share your story. These are general guidelines, and like most rules, there may be exceptions. But in general, these guidelines hold true:

• Try to keep your story conversational and brief.

• You should be able to share each of your testimonies in 3 to 5 minutes. Nobody likes someone who hogs the conversation speaking about themselves.

• Don't worry so much about saying it "right." Say it "real." Be yourself. This isn't speech class or a sermon. Share from your heart and put the spotlight on Jesus.

• Practice enough so that you are comfortable sharing your story with someone who needs to know Jesus.

• As you share, try to avoid religious terminology that an unchurched person may not understand clearly. To do this, use the definition of the word instead of the word (e.g. instead of "repented" say "I turned from going my own way to follow Jesus").

• It's not usually appropriate to share sordid details. People don't usually want to know. For example, instead of saying, "I was so broken and lonely that I was sleeping with a different person every night. I got several STDs, but I didn't even care", try something like, "I was broken and lonely. I was with lots of different people, desperately looking for someone to fill the void, which only led to more pain and problems."

• Keep the emphasis on the difference that Jesus had made in your life.

• You can adjust the details you include in your story according to what would connect most with the person(s) to whom you are speaking. For example, if you know the person you're talking to is an addict, you would want to emphasize parts of your story that could connect with them at that level. Or if the person you are speaking to is an un-born again church goer, then you'd want to emphasize parts of your story that would help them understand having a personal relationship with Jesus.

• Don't be afraid to be vulnerable. We are bearing witness of the difference Jesus makes in our lives, His goodness, not our own.

• If you were converted at an early age and have followed Jesus Christ faithfully, you still have an amazing testimony of the difference Jesus makes in your life. Since you don't have a "before Christ", focus on what your life is like when you aren't living in the Spirit.

• If you've had periods of "backsliding", rather than telling a chronological story that might confuse someone about the gospel,. lump everything into categories- your life apart from Jesus, how you realized the grace of Jesus, and the difference Jesus makes.

TESTIMONY WORKSHEET:

Use this outline to structure your story. Jot a few notes under each category. It's not necessary to write your entire story. Just make a few notes to jog your memory for learning to share it as part of a conversation.

BEFORE/WITHOUT CHRIST-

REALIZATION/CONVERSION-

DIFFERENCE/CHANGE-

OPENING AND CLOSING THE DOOR FOR YOUR TESTIMONIES

It's very easy to share your testimony effectively when you know how to open the door for your testimony and how to close your testimony effectively. Here are some simple examples of using different approaches to opening the door.

After you read them, put a circle around the one that you think you will use most comfortably, or make up your own in the blank space below:

> Video 5.2
> (8 min.)
>
> **Opening & Closing the Door for Jesus Stories**

- "I used to have that same problem. Let me share something that has made a huge difference in my life. Okay?"

- "I know something that has made a real difference in my life that I know would help you too. I'd love to tell you more, if you are interested."

- "Why am I always so happy? Do you really want to know? I wasn't always, but something really changed my life. You want to hear about it?

- "I've found something that has made a huge difference in my life that I think you'd be interested in. Can I tell you about it?"

- "I've known you for a long time, and you know I'm a Christian, but that means a lot of different things to different people. It would mean a lot to me if I could share with you what this means to me. Can I?"

- Have you ever experienced God? You can! Let me share how I began experiencing God constantly.

- _____

_____

Finally, when you are done with your story (and you should try to keep it less than 5 minutes) you'll want to close by asking a question to invite your friend to respond to you.

Here are some of my favorite closing questions. Circle the one you believe you will use the most:

- Has anything like this ever happened to you?
- Do you understand how Jesus Christ can do the same thing for you?
- Do you know how you can experience God like this?

III. LOOK OUT:
PRACTICE
1. Grab a partner for role play
a. Share your "bullet stories" in response to the following scenario:

A co-worker was talking about a movie in which one of the characters was confused, broken, and dysfunctional. Then they jokingly say to you, "Not that you'd know anything about that. They don't have it all together like you."

b. Switch roles and allow your partner to share their bullet stories.

c. Give feedback. What was good? What could make it even better?

d. Repeat and incorporate the feedback.

2. a. Practice sharing your "Jesus SALVATION story" with your partner.

b. Switch roles and allow your partner to share their salvation story.

c. Give and receive feedback. What was good? What could make it even better?

d. Incorporate feedback and repeat. This time, practice opening and closing the door to your story by using the phrases you circled on the previous page. Be sure to keep it under five minutes.

PLAN

1. Make a list of the people that you believe you could share your salvation story to practice: Don't overlook the obvious- saved friends, your children, your spouse, etc. Make a quick list.

2. Make a goal to share your salvation story as much as possible this week so that you get very comfortable sharing it with others. What is your goal (stretch yourself!)?

3. Who really needs to hear your testimonies? Make a list in the space below. Next, circle the one or two names that you want to purpose to share your story with this week. Plan to report back next week how it went.

PRAY

a. Tell your group the name of the person(s) you plan to share your testimony with this week so you can all pray for them together.

b. If anyone needs healing or prayer, lay hands and minister to one another.

.

CHAPTER 6
IMMERSED IN GOD (PART 2)

I. LOOK BACK-
A. How have you experienced God at work in you this past week? Share any highlights, lessons, insights or encouragement.

B. How have you experienced God at work through you to touch others this past week? Did you share your testimony with others this week? What happened when you shared your testimony? Were there others ways you stepped out to demonstrate the Kingdom of God to others this week? What did you experience? Share any highlights or challenges.

II. LESSON
UNDERSTANDING YOUR SPIRIT
In order to grasp your union with Jesus Christ, you must understand the unique features of your spirit, your soul, and your body.

1) In the Scriptures below,
a. UNDERLINE the phrases that refer to your spirit and/or your union with Christ in the spirit
b. CIRCLE the phrases that refer to your soul (your mind, emotions/desires, and will)
c. SHADE the phrases that refer to your body
d. ANSWER any questions based on the verses directly preceding the question.

Now may the God of peace himself sanctify you completely, and may your whole spirit and soul and body be kept blameless at the coming of our Lord Jesus Christ. 1 Thes.5:23

In that day (when the Holy Spirit is sent) *you will know that I* (Jesus) *am in my Father, and you in me, and I in you. John14:20*

If Jesus is in the Father, and you are in Jesus, how do you look to the Father?

If Jesus is in the Father and inside of you, how close are you to God?

Is it possible to know these things *by experience* instead of just "theory"? If so, how?

For those whom he foreknew he also predestined to be conformed to the image of his Son, in order that he might be the firstborn among many brothers. And those whom he predestined he also called, and those whom he called he also justified, and those whom he justified he also glorified. Rom 8:29-30

When did God first know you?

What is the significance of God saying that you are" glorified"(past tense)?

But he who is joined to the Lord is one spirit with Him. 1Co 6:17

If it was the Spirit of Jesus Christ that made Him amazing, what does that mean for you?

For by a single offering he has perfected for all time those who are being sanctified. Heb 10:14

What did the offering of Jesus Christ make you? For how long?

Fill in the blank— Because of the blood of Jesus Christ, I am_____ even while my life is being set apart for God.

Now SAY IT! (God does!)

If then you have been raised with Christ, seek the things that are above, where Christ is, seated at the right hand of God. Set your minds on things that are above, not on things that are on earth. For you have died, and your life is hidden with Christ in God. When Christ who is your life appears, then you also will appear with him in glory. Col 3:1-4

Are believers waiting to be raised up with Christ one day, or have they already been raised up with Christ?

Who is your life?

Does God really believe that Christ IS *YOUR* life? Do you?

But God, being rich in mercy, because of the great love with which he loved us, even when we were dead in our trespasses, made us alive together with Christ--by grace you have been saved--and raised us up with him and seated us with him in the heavenly places in Christ Jesus, Eph 2:4-7

Where are you?

What are you doing way up there?

When you pray, are you striving to get where God already put you, or enjoying the view?

And because you are sons, God has sent the Spirit of his Son into our hearts, crying, "Abba! Father!" So you are no longer a slave, but a son, and if a son, then an heir through God. Gal. 4:6-7

How can this help you the next time you feel emotionally distant from God?

Put off your old self, which belongs to your former manner of life and is corrupt through deceitful desires, and to be renewed in the spirit of your minds, and to put on the new self, created after the likeness of God in true righteousness and holiness. Eph 4:22-24

What do we do with our old self — improve it, or just put it off?

Do you need to improve your new self or just put Him on?

Who does your new-self look like?

So we do not lose heart. Though our outer self is wasting away, our inner self is being renewed day by day. For this light momentary affliction is preparing for us an eternal weight of glory beyond all comparison, as we look not to the things that are seen but to the things that are unseen. For the things that are seen are transient, but the things that are unseen are eternal. 2Co 4:16-18

When we fix our eyes on what is unseen, what happens?

Do not present your members to sin as instruments for unrighteousness, but present yourselves to God as those that are alive from the dead, and your members to God as instruments for righteousness. Rom 6:13

When you present yourself to God, how do you present yourself?

But if Christ is in you, although the body is dead because of sin, the Spirit is life because of righteousness. If the Spirit of him who raised Jesus from the dead dwells in you, he who raised Christ Jesus from the dead will also give life to your mortal bodies through his Spirit who dwells in you. Rom. 8:10-11

What is the relationship between our body and the Holy Spirit?

You are perfect in your spirit because your spirit is one with Jesus Christ. You are being transformed in your soul, which includes your mind, your emotions and desires, and your will. Your body is a container of your soul and your spirit. As you are filled with the Holy Spirit, through your body, the Spirit of God is made manifest in this world.

You function in the Spirit as you exercise FAITH, HOPE, and LOVE in the VICTORY and POWER of the Lord Jesus Christ.

HABITS TO CULTIVATE A LIFESTYLE OF FELLOWSHIP WITH GOD
God has removed the separation between "secular" and "spiritual." Our entire lives, "whether we eat or drink, or whatever we do" is now part of our relationship with God. It's all included into our fellowship with God. Our lives are immersed in God. When we work, "we work as unto the Lord." Every relationship, whether within our family, or friends, neighbors or even persecutors, has now become an opportunity to live in fellowship with God.

In this lesson we will introduce 2 Habits to cultivate lifestyle of fellowship with God.

1) Make every day a running conversation with God.

In the Scriptures below:
a. UNDERLINE instructions about HOW, WHEN, or WHERE we can pray.
b. CIRCLE the benefits and results of cultivating a lifestyle of fellowship with God.

Lead me in your truth and teach me, for you are the God of my salvation; for you I wait all the day long. Psalm 25:5

Pray without ceasing. 1 Thes. 5:17

praying at all times in the Spirit, with all prayer and supplication. To that end keep alert with all perseverance, making supplication for all the saints, Eph 6:18

But stay awake at all times, praying that you may have strength to escape all these things that are going to take place, and to stand before the Son of Man." Luk 21:36

Because you are sons, God has sent the Spirit of his Son into our hearts, crying, "Abba! Father!" Gal 4:5-6

Does the Spirit of Jesus Christ ever stop fellowshipping with the Father inside of you?

How can that help us understand true prayer? Is it something we do, or something we become aware of and participate in?

How does this make continual fellowship with God a practical experience that empowers us rather than a frustrating impossibility?

2) Call on the Name of the Lord- touching God with a single breath.

In the Scriptures below:
a. UNDERLINE instructions about HOW, WHEN, or WHERE we can call on the Name of the Lord

b. CIRCLE the benefits and results of cultivating a lifestyle of fellowship with God by calling on the Name of the Lord.

To the church of God that is in Corinth, to those sanctified in Christ Jesus, called to be saints together with all those who in every place call upon the name of our Lord Jesus Christ, both their Lord and ours. 1 Cor. 1:2

So flee youthful passions and pursue righteousness, faith, love, and peace, along with those who call on the Lord from a pure heart. 2 Tim.2:22

… For the same Lord is Lord of all, bestowing his riches on all who call on him. Rom 10:12

For you, O Lord, are good and forgiving, abounding in steadfast love to all who call upon you… In the day of my trouble I call upon you, for you answer me.. Psalm 86:5,7

Therefore I want you to understand that no one speaking in the Spirit of God ever says "Jesus is accursed!" and no one can say "Jesus is Lord" except in the Holy Spirit. 1Co 12:3

What did you learn about the benefits of a calling upon the Name of the Lord?

III. LOOK OUT
PRACTICE
1. Break into groups of 3 or 4 to practice "calling on the Name of the Lord."
Get comfortable and close together. You can join hands if you wish. Close your eyes and turn your attention to the Lord's presence. At the start of this exercise, close your eyes and pay attention to how you feel. Now, begin to call on the Name of the Lord together. Call upon His Name in Love and in faith that His presence is inside you and among you. His favor is towards you. Pay attention to His presence together. Do nothing else. No requests. No confession. No long sentences. Just call on His Name in faith and love and enjoy His presence together. Do this for 5 minutes.

2. Discussion: What do you observe about the difference between your awareness of how you felt spiritually at start of this exercise vs. the end of this exercise? What did you enjoy most from this exercise?

PLAN

1. This week you will begin to cultivate a lifestyle of fellowship with God by developing the habits we discussed in this lesson:

> ➤ Make each day a running conversation with the Lord.

> ➤ Call on the Name of the Lord.

b. Take a walk with Jesus this week. Make it a date. As you walk with Him, call on His Name and speak to Him about the things you see around you. Find as many ways to enjoy Him as you can.

PRAY

a. Pray for one another. Ask God to make you a people of continual fellowship with Him and awareness of His presence.

b. If anyone needs healing or prayer, lay hands and minister to one another.

CHAPTER 7
SHARING YOUR JESUS STORIES
PART 2

I. LOOK BACK-
A. How have you experienced God at work in you this past week? Share any highlights, lessons, insights or encouragement.

B. How have you experienced God at work through you to touch others this past week? How have you taken steps of faith to demonstrate the Kingdom of God to others this week? What did you experience? Share any highlights or challenges.

II. LESSON

QUICK REVIEW
Previously we learned:
- How to share our "Bullet Testimonies"- simple one or two line snapshots that share how Jesus changed your life.
- Salvation Testimony with a simple framework- 1) Without Christ, 2) How your eyes were opened to Christ, and 3)the difference Jesus makes in your life.
- Opening and Closing the Door for your testimonies.

As a review, share an example of each:

➤ Bullet Testimony
➤ Salvation Testimony, and
➤ Opening and Closing the Door for your testimony

UNLEASHING THE POWER OF YOUR TESTIMONIES
Testimonies are effective ways to connect with people, to identify yourself with the mindsets of the people with whom you are speaking. Instead of correcting them directly, you can share your story starting from the point that you had similar mindsets, struggles, and approaches to life as the person to whom you are speaking. As you share how you discovered the reality of Jesus Christ and the difference He makes in your life, you can bring them along the path that you've walked to discover life in the Kingdom. As they see life through your story, they have the opportunity to see past their own barriers without feeling "preached at" or "talked-down-to."

We will begin this lesson with a short study on Biblical principles for communication. Then we will develop additional kinds of testimonies so that you will be ready to speak about the difference that Jesus Christ makes in your life with a great deal of flexibility in almost any conversation.

SPEAKING LIFE AND BUILDING BRIDGES

1) In the following Scriptures,
a. UNDERLINE phrases that indicate mindsets and practices we should AVOID.
b. CIRCLE phrases that indicate mindsets and practices we should ADOPT.

A fool's lips walk into a fight, and his mouth invites a beating. Pro 18:6

We know that "all of us possess knowledge." This "knowledge" puffs up, but love builds up. 1 Cor.8:1

> **Video 7.1**
> **(2 min.)**
>
> **Connect with People to Communicate Christ**

If one gives an answer before he hears, it is his folly and shame. Pro 18:13

A word fitly spoken is like apples of gold in a setting of silver. Like a gold ring or an ornament of gold is a wise reprover to a listening ear. Pro 25:11-12

And the Lord's servant must not be quarrelsome but kind to everyone, able to teach, patiently enduring evil, correcting his opponents with gentleness. 2 Tim. 2:24-25

Death and life are in the power of the tongue, and those who love it will eat its fruits. Pro 18:21

1) What are some of the ways that you see these principles embodied in life of Jesus Christ?

2) What are some of the ways that we can apply these principles to help us to use our testimonies more effectively to demonstrate the Kingdom of God?

SHARING YOUR "JESUS POWER STORIES"

The testimony framework that we used to share our salvation story works well to share other kinds of Jesus stories, like how you discovered the power of Jesus Christ was available to work through you today. In the body of Christ, we need many people sharing these testimonies to shut the mouth of the accuser of the brothers, who would want to make us believe that God's power has left the earth. People need to hear your story and you should be prepared to share.

> **Video 7.2**
> **(4 min.)**
>
> **Sharing Your Jesus "Power Story"**

BEFORE/WITHOUT:- What were your mindsets and experiences before you discovered that the power of Jesus Christ would operate through you today?.

REALIZATION/CONVERSION: What changed your mind? How did you discover that Jesus Christ operates in His power through us today?

DIFFERENCE/CHANGE: How have you seen the power of God make a difference in your life or the lives of others? What have you seen Jesus Christ do through you and others you know personally?

Use the testimony worksheet on the following page to develop your "Jesus Power" story.

TESTIMONY WORKSHEET- JESUS POWER STORY:

Use this outline to structure your story. Jot a few notes under each category. It's not necessary to write your entire story. Just make a few notes to jog your memory for learning to share it as part of a conversation.

BEFORE/WITHOUT THE POWER OF JESUS CHRIST-

REALIZATION/CONVERSION-

DIFFERENCE/CHANGE-

STRATEGIC STORY

With your testimonies, you'll be surprised how many opportunities you'll find to speak to others about Jesus Christ. You don't have to wait around for someone to come up to you asking, "What must I do to be saved?" to be able to release the power of God in your testimony.

Video 7.3
(8 min.)

You ALWAYS have a Story

1) Brainstorm Exercise:

In the space provided below, jot down as many areas of life that you've experienced Jesus Christ making a difference in your life. Take 5 minutes to write down as many areas that you can remember. I've gotten your list started with "Overcoming Fear", "Handling Pressure at Work", and "Marriage". See how many you can come up with yourself:

Overcoming Fear

Handling Pressure at Work

Marriage

2) a. Review the brainstorm list you created. Cross out any subject that you believe it would be too difficult for you to share a story of how Jesus Christ has made a difference in your life.

b. Review the list that remains from your brainstorm. How does it make you feel to realize that ANY TIME you are in a conversation that touches on any one of these subjects, God can use you to share a powerful witness for Jesus Christ?

3) From the brainstorm exercise above, CIRCLE one subject to develop into a third testimony, which we will call your "STRATEGIC STORY".

To select your strategic story, think about what you bring to the table for the people that you are around every day. For example, if you are working in the business world, you may want to develop a story about the difference that life in Christ makes as you handle pressure at work. If you are a mom, you may want to develop a story about the difference Jesus makes in your life as a mom. If you've had a significant battle with depression and anxiety, you can share about the difference that Jesus Christ made in helping you overcome depression and anxiety.

Once you've selected the subject for your Strategic Story, use the testimony worksheet on the following page to develop your story.

TESTIMONY WORKSHEET- STRATEGIC STORY:

Use this outline to structure your strategic story. Jot a few notes under each category. It's not necessary to write your entire story. Just make a few notes to jog your memory for learning to share it as part of a conversation.

BEFORE/WITHOUT THE POWER OF JESUS CHRIST-

REALIZATION/CONVERSION-

DIFFERENCE/CHANGE-

III. LOOK OUT:

PRACTICE:

A. Partner Up and Practice your new stories. For each time you share, open the door for your story and close the door.

    1. a. Share your Jesus Power Story with one another

    b. Get and give feedback to one another. What was good? What could make it even better?

    c. Incorporate the feedback and repeat.

    2. a. Share your Strategic Story with one another

    b. Get and give feedback to one another. What was good? What could make it even better?

    c. Incorporate the feedback and repeat.

PLAN

1. Make a plan to practice sharing your Jesus Power Story and Strategic Story with friends and family. Who can you "practice" with? Set a goal to share your stories. How many times do you want to practice sharing your new stories this week?

2. Often we are connected with believers who don't walk in the power of Jesus Christ. God can use you to help them. Who do you know that needs to hear your Jesus Power Story?

Make a plan to connect with them and share your story?

3. Who do you know that needs to hear your Strategic Story?

Make a plan to connect with them and share your story?

PRAY

If anyone needs healing or prayer, lay hands and minister to one another

CHAPTER 8
HEALING THE SICK LIKE JESUS

I. LOOK BACK-
A. How have you experienced **God at work *in you*** this past week? Share any highlights, lessons, insights or encouragement.

B. How have you experienced **God at work *through you*** to touch others this past week? How did your assignment to share your power story and strategic story? What did you experience? Share any highlights or challenges.

II. LESSON
In this lesson you will learn how to heal the sick like Jesus Christ.

Some Christians come from backgrounds where they were taught that God no longer intends to work in His miraculous power through believers today, because now we have the Bible. They suppose that miracles were needed only to validate the Bible, and once the Bible's authority is established miracles are no longer needed. Because they hold to this view, anyone who claims that God is working through them to heal the sick is treated with a great deal of suspicion and sometimes outright hostility, since in their view, this would give them authority to speak for God like the original New Testament writers. There's one BIG problem with this though... this view is never taught in the Bible... ***anywhere***! In fact, the Bible specifically teaches otherwise.

1) Read the verses below.
a. UNDERLINE every phrase that indicates WHO God expects to heal the sick
b. CIRCLE those phrases that indicates HOW believers heal the sick like Jesus.
c. ANSWER the questions following each of the verses below based on the verse immediately above the question.

So Jesus said to them, "Truly, truly, I say to you, the Son can do nothing of his own accord, but only what he sees the Father doing. For whatever the Father does, that the Son does in like manner. John 5:19

Could Jesus do miracles on His own accord?

What did Jesus see the Father doing? Leaving people sick, making people sick, or healing the sick?

Truly, truly, I say to you, whoever believes in me will also do the works that I do; and greater works than these will he do, because I am going to the Father. John 14:12

Who does Jesus say will do the same works He did and even greater?

A disciple is not above his teacher, but everyone when he is fully trained will be like his teacher. Luke 6:40

What is the end result of being fully trained by Jesus?

And he said to them, "Go into all the world and proclaim the gospel to the whole creation. Whoever believes and is baptized will be saved… and these signs will accompany those who believe: in my name they will cast out demons; they will speak in new tongues; they will pick up serpents with their hands; and if they drink any deadly poison, it will not hurt them; they will lay their hands on the sick, and they will recover." Mark 16:15-18

Who does Jesus say will have signs following them— apostles, or those who believe what the gospel the apostles preached?

'Lord, Lord, did we not prophesy in your name, and cast out demons in your name, and do many mighty works in your name?' And Jesus will declare to them, 'I never knew you; depart from me, you workers of lawlessness.' Matt. 7:21-23

What does this teach us about the source of our spiritual identity? Is it miracles through us or Christ in us? Why is this important?

If Jesus doesn't deny that even the unconverted can do miracles in His Name, do you think miracles may also be possible for a true child of God?

When Peter saw it he addressed the people: "Men of Israel, why do you wonder at this, or why do you stare at us, as though by our own power or piety we have made him walk? The God of Abraham, the God of Isaac, and the God of Jacob, the God of our fathers, glorified his servant Jesus…And His name--by faith in his name--has made this man strong whom you see and know, and the faith that is through Jesus has given the man this perfect health in the presence of you all. Act 3:11-16

Did Peter attribute his miracles to the fact he was an apostle?

To each is given the manifestation of the Spirit for the common good. For to one is given through the Spirit the utterance of wisdom, and to another the utterance of knowledge according to the same Spirit, to another faith by the same Spirit, to another gifts of healing by the one Spirit, to another the working of miracles, to another prophecy, to another the ability to distinguish between spirits, to another various kinds of tongues, to another the interpretation of tongues. All these are empowered by one and the same Spirit, who apportions to each one individually as he wills. 1Co 12:7-11

Was the Corinthian church a solid church or a messed up church?

Did the apostle Paul believe that God was doing real miracles and healings through the Corinthian believers?

How might this both encourage and warn believers today?

Does he who supplies the Spirit to you and works miracles among you do so by works of the law, or by hearing with faith? Gal 3:5

Did Paul assume that the churches in Galatia experiencing miracles? Why?

How do we experience miracles— by living up to God's standards or by having faith in the gospel of Jesus Christ?

How might this explain how some ministers have been used mightily yet fallen in scandal?

And the crowds with one accord paid attention to what was being said by Philip when they heard him and saw the signs that he did. For unclean spirits, crying out with a loud voice, came out of many who had them, and many who were paralyzed or lame were healed. Acts. 8:6-7

Was God doing miracles through Philip? What was his role in the Jerusalem church (read Acts 6:2-5)?

And he called the twelve together and gave them power and authority over all demons and to cure diseases, and he sent them out to proclaim the kingdom of God and to heal. Luke 9:1-2

Did Jesus ever send anyone out to proclaim the gospel with words alone? Why?

After this the Lord appointed seventy-two others and sent them on ahead of him, two by two, into every town and place where he himself was about to go. Heal the sick in it and say to them, 'The kingdom of God has come near to you.' Luke10:1,9

Was Jesus demonstrating that a supernatural life of miracles was exclusive to the apostles or for all His disciples?

And Jesus came and said to them, "All authority in heaven and on earth has been given to me. Go therefore and make disciples of all nations, baptizing them in the name of the Father and of the Son and of the Holy Spirit, teaching them to observe all that I have commanded you. And behold, I am with you always, to the end of the age." Matt. 28:18-20

Did Jesus command the disciples to heal the sick, cast out demons, and raise the dead?

According to Matt. 28:18-20, should disciples be taught to obey these commands today?

CORRECTING TWO COMMON MISTAKES THAT HINDER HEALING

Christians make two common mistakes regarding healing: 1) Many Christians teach that sickness is sometimes God's will, and 2) When it comes to healing, many Christians continue to act like beggars, asking God to do what He's told us to do in the power He's already provided.

Sometimes Christians say things like, "It's not always God's will to heal" or "They'll be healed in God's perfect timing" or "Please heal my friend, if it be Thy will." Let's examine statements like these in view of the gospel of the Kingdom revealed in Jesus Christ.

IS SICKNESS AND DISEASE EVER GOD'S WILL?

Did Jesus Christ ever treat sickness or disease like it was God's will or part of God's plan for people? Is sickness God's will or the devil's? Let's look at the Scriptures.

Fix your faith upon the Word of God until your life looks like the Word.

---

a. UNDERLINE every phrase that indicates how Jesus Christ treated sickness.
b. CIRCLE those phrases that indicates that it is the Father's will to heal sickness and disease.
c. ANSWER any questions based on the verse immediately preceding the question.

God anointed Jesus of Nazareth with the Holy Spirit and with power. He went about doing good and healing all who were oppressed by the devil, for God was with him. Act 10:38

Did Jesus ever fail to heal anyone away who needed healing?

Did Jesus Christ view sickness as the will of God or the work of the devil?

Was Jesus healing by His own divine power, or was He depending upon the power of the Holy Spirit like believers do today?

That evening they brought to him many who were oppressed by demons, and he cast out the spirits with a word and healed all who were sick. Mat 8:16

Did Jesus turn any away who needed healing?

Did Jesus ever say, "Sorry, you are just like Job. You'll need to stay sick a while longer while my Father works out His mysterious plan in your life?"

And he went throughout all Galilee, teaching in their synagogues and proclaiming the gospel of the kingdom and healing every disease and every affliction among the people. So his fame spread throughout all Syria, and they brought him all the sick, those afflicted with various diseases and pains, those oppressed by demons, epileptics, and paralytics, and he healed them. Mat 4:23-24

Did Jesus blame people for their sickness? Did Jesus blame God for sickness?

Jesus said to him, "…Whoever has seen me has seen the Father." John 14:9

"Then you will know that I am He, and that I do nothing on my own authority, but speak just as the Father taught me. And He who sent me is with me. He has not left me alone, for I always do the things that are pleasing to Him." John8:28-29

Do you not believe that I am in the Father and the Father is in me?...The Father who dwells in me does his works. Believe me that I am in the Father and the Father is in me, or else believe on account of the works themselves. Truly, truly, I say to you, whoever believes in me will also do the works that I do; and greater works than these will he do, because I am going to the Father. John 14:10-12

If Jesus is our clearest and most complete picture of God, do we see Jesus Christ making people sick?

Do we see Him leaving people sick who came to Him for healing?

Think it through…

If a Christian commits a sin, is that God's will?

In order to walk in victory over sin, do they need God to give them something more? Or do they need to learn to walk in what God has accomplished and provided for them through the cross?

Jesus Christ has provided all we need for holiness AND healing.

Surely he has borne our griefs and carried our sorrows; yet we esteemed him stricken, smitten by God, and afflicted. But he was pierced for our transgressions; he was crushed for our iniquities; upon him was the chastisement that brought us peace, and with his wounds we are healed. All we like sheep have gone astray; we have turned—every one—to his own way; and the LORD has laid on him the iniquity of us all. Isa 53:4-

BEGGERS OR SONS?

Do we need to ask God to do something more or to give us something more in order for healing to take place? Or do we need to do what He's already told us to do and appropriate the power He has provided?

Let's examine the Scriptures.
a. **UNDERLINE** every phrase that indicates that God has given believers the authority to act as His representatives to heal the sick.
b. **CIRCLE** every phrase that indicates God expects us to heal the sick, not just take care of them and encourage them.
c. **ANSWER** the questions following each of the verses below based on the verse immediately above the question.

> *But Peter said, "I have no silver and gold, but what I do have I give to you. In the name of Jesus Christ of Nazareth, rise up and walk!"* Act 3:6

Did Peter need to ask God to release more power? Or did he believe he had the authority to give to others what God had already given us through Christ?

Was the lame man healed because he had faith or because Peter had faith for his healing?

Surely he has borne our sickness and carried our pains… But he was pierced for our transgressions; he was crushed for our iniquities; upon him was the chastisement that brought us peace, and with his wounds we are healed. Isa 53:3-5

He touched her hand, and the fever left her, and she rose and began to serve him. That evening they brought to him many who were oppressed by demons, and he cast out the spirits with a word and healed all who were sick. This was to fulfill what was spoken by the prophet Isaiah: "He took our illnesses and bore our diseases." Mat 8:15-17

Did Jesus Christ suffer only for our forgiveness or also for healing in our body and soul?

Healing the sick is normal Christianity for all believers, because healing the sick is normal for Jesus Christ who lives inside of them.

And proclaim as you go, saying, 'The kingdom of heaven is at hand.' Heal the sick, raise the dead, cleanse lepers, cast out demons. You received without paying; give without pay. Mat 10:7-8

Do we need to receive a special leading to heal the sick? Or can we just act on the authority of Jesus' command?

Should a gospel minister ever ask people for a financial donation towards their healing? Or did Jesus Christ purchase our healing through the stripes on His back? Why is this important?

And when they came to the crowd, a man came up to him and, kneeling before him, said, "Lord, have mercy on my son, for he is an epileptic and he suffers terribly. For often he falls into the fire, and often into the water. And I brought him to your disciples, and they could not heal him." And Jesus answered, "O faithless and twisted generation, how long am I to be with you? How long am I to bear with you? Bring him here to me." And Jesus rebuked the demon, and it came out of him, and the boy was healed instantly. Then the disciples came to Jesus privately and said, "Why could we not cast it out?" He said to them, "Because of your little faith. For truly, I say to you, if you have faith like a grain of mustard seed, you will say to this mountain, 'Move from here to there,' and it will move, and nothing will be impossible for you." Mat 17:14-20

Did the disciples have the authority and power needed to heal the boy?

Did they get the boy healed?

Was it God's will to heal the boy or to leave the boy sick and oppressed?

Was God the cause of the boy not being healed? Or was it the boy or the boy's father? Or was it the doubt in the hearts and minds of the disciples?

Is anyone among you sick? Let him call for the elders of the church, and let them pray over him, anointing him with oil in the name of the Lord. And the prayer (lit.- "vow") of faith will save the one who is sick, and the Lord will raise him up. And if he has committed sins, he will be forgiven. Jas 5:14-15

Does God expect us to accept sickness or fight sickness by faith?

Does God expect that a believer who has committed sins will be healed by the prayer of faith?

Does God expect church leaders to encourage the sick, accuse the sick, or to heal the sick?

Summary: Christians walk in union with Jesus Christ. We must renew our minds to adopt His mindset and attitude towards sickness and disease. Jesus always treated sickness as a work of the enemy that was subject to Him. In order to minister healing, Christians should lay hands on the sick, command sickness and affliction to leave, and the body to be healed in the Name of Jesus Christ.

> **Video 8.2**
> **(20 min.)**
>
> **Making the Most of**
> **Every Opportunity**

III. LOOK OUT
PRACTICE

1. Review the basic outline to healing ministry together. Someone who is experienced should demonstrate each step.

1. Approach
2. Ask
3. Minister
4. Test
5. Rejoice or Repeat
6. Connect and Close

1. **Approach**: Go to people. Build rapport quickly with a pleasant demeanor. Take as much time to building rapport as you feel is appropriate or necessary.

2. **Ask:** Say something like, "I noticed you were walking with a cane and thought, you're too young and good looking to be using a cane. What happened? Do you have pain?" Or, if there is no visible condition like a cane, crutch, or an oxygen tank, you can say, "This may sound crazy, but I was wondering if you have anything that causes pain in your body? God uses me to set people free from pain and I just felt like I should ask you."

3. **Minister:** Tell them. "I can help you with that. Are you ready for that pain to go?" While holding out your hand like you're asking for money, say "Let me see your hand for a second" They'll put their hand in yours automatically, even if they are wondering what you are about to do. Then grasp their hand firmly (but not hard enough to hurt them), and minister healing, "Father, thank you for all you've done. In Jesus' Name, pain/sickness, Go now. Be healed. I set you free in Jesus' Name"

4. **Test:** Then immediately say, "Now test that out. Move it around and tell me what's changed."

5. **Rejoice or Repeat:** Rejoice in their healing or Repeat the process, by saying, "Sometimes I pray more than once. Let's hit this again quickly." Then take their hands and command healing once more.

6. **Connect and Close:** When it's time to wrap up your spontaneous healing ministry, you will have experienced perceptible change or not. Regardless, maintain your confidence in God and love for people. You may want to offer contact information or additional resources to people who seem open to more.

2. Role Play: Break up in pairs and practice ministering to a stranger with pain. One person should take the role of the infirm person, and the other person takes the role of the minister. Go through this exercise by breaking down the steps and adding one more step each time:

> a. Practice Approach
> b. Approach and Ask
> c. Approach, ask and Minister
> d. Approach, ask, minister, test
> e. Approach, ask, minister, test, rejoice/repeat
> f. Then finally put it all together with a Connect/Close

Each time, you repeat all the previous steps and add one more. This will give you lots of repetition on the early steps, but I've found that the beginning steps are the most important to get comfortable with. The repetition will help you gain confidence and comfort.

Then switch roles and allow your partner to practice going through all the steps.

PLAN

1. Who do you know that has sickness or pain in their body? Make an appointment to go and minister to them.

2. Pick a store and go and minister to as many employees as you can. Approach them and build a little rapport. Then ask them, "You are working hard, and I've found that a lot of people are having to work in spite of how they feel. Do you have anything that gives you pain or trouble at all in your body? Anything at all?" Then take the conversation from there. You can do this with a partner.

Write your plan here:
        Where?
        When?
        With whom?

PRAY

If anyone needs healing or prayer, lay hands and minister to one another.

CHAPTER 9
SPEAKING SUPERNATURAL
WORDS OF ENCOURAGEMENT
AND DIVINE INSIGHT (PART 1)

I. LOOK BACK-
A. How have you experienced **God at work** *in you* this past week? Share any highlights, lessons, insights or encouragement..

B. How have you experienced **God at work** *through you* to touch others this past week? How did your assignment go to minister to people you knew and to employees at a store? What did you experience? Share any highlights or challenges.

II. LESSON
God wants to speak very personally into people's lives through you. It's one of the ways He reveals Himself today. Because Jesus Christ lives in you, He can speak through you into the lives of others in very powerful ways.

> **Video 9.1**
> **(17 min.)**
>
> **Learning to**
> **Speak from God**

1) In the following Scriptures,
a. UNDERLINE phrases that indicate WHO can speak spontaneous words that flow from the Spirit of God

b. CIRCLE phrases that indicate what we can do to cooperate with God in allowing Him to use us to speak to people through us.

"'And in the last days it shall be, God declares, that I will pour out my Spirit on all flesh, and your sons and your daughters shall prophesy, and your young men shall see visions, and your old men shall dream dreams; even on my male servants and female servants in those days I will pour out my Spirit, and they shall prophesy. Act 2:17-18

Whoever speaks, speak as one who speaks oracles of God 1Pe 4:11

Pursue love, and earnestly desire the spiritual gifts, especially that you may prophesy. 1Co 14:1

On the other hand, the one who prophesies speaks to people for their up building and encouragement and consolation. 1Co 14:3

Let two or three prophets speak, and let the others weigh what is said. If a revelation is made to another sitting there, let the first be silent. For you can all prophesy one by one, so that all may learn and all be encouraged, 1Co 14:29-31

For the testimony of Jesus is the spirit of prophecy. Rev. 19:10
Based on these verses above:

JESUS AND PROPHETIC EVANGELISM

Jesus demonstrated how He used spoke prophetically in His personal ministry on many occasions. For example, with Nathaniel. *Nathanael said to him, "Can anything good come out of Nazareth?" Philip said to him, "Come and see." Jesus saw Nathanael coming toward him and said of him, "Behold,* **an Israelite indeed, in whom there is no deceit***!" Nathanael said to him, "How do you know me?" Jesus answered him,* **"Before Philip called you, when you were under the fig tree, I saw you***." Nathanael answered him, "Rabbi, you are the Son of God! You are the King of Israel!" Jesus answered him, "Because I said to you, 'I saw you under the fig tree,' do you believe? You will see greater things than these." And he said to him,* **"Truly, truly, I say to you, you will see heaven opened, and the angels of God ascending and descending on the Son of Man***." Jn 1:46-51*

How did Jesus speak into Nathaniel's life?

What impact did this have on Nathaniel?

Was Nathaniel saved yet or born again? What does this show us about how God speaks to sinners?

DISCUSSION: "What are some ways God has spoken into your life personally through others?"

SPEAKING TO THE LOST SONS-

In Luke 15, the Pharisees and scribes murmured, saying, "This man receives sinners, and eats with them. And Jesus spoke 3 spontaneous stories over these lost sinners.

How did the Shepherd feel about the Lost Sheep?

What did he do to find the sheep?

What did he do once He recovered His lost sheep?

Video 9.2
(10 min.)

Prophetic Evangelism

How did the woman who had lost the silver coin feel about the lost coin?

What did she do when she realized the coin was lost?

What did she do once she recovered the coin?

How did the Father feel about His lost son?

What did the Father say to the older brother?

What did the Father do once the son returned?

What do these stories show us about how and what God speaks to those who do not yet know the Father's destiny for them or His heart for them?

How did Jesus' interaction with Nathaniel demonstrate these same principles?

When you want to speak into someone's life, allow the Father speak as He speaks to "lost sons" through you. Some are lost prodigals, others are upset "older brothers",

others are "home" and need encouragement, up building and consolation as they walk as faithful sons and daughters.

PRACTICAL KEYS:
Let God speak through you by

➢ Asking God to help you see every person through His eyes so He can speak through you.

➢ Asking God to show you, "What are they like?"

➢ Asking God about, "What are they good at?"

➢ Asking God to show you, "What do you want to do in their lives that they may not realize?"

You can open doors to speak into people's life with these phrases like these:

➢ *"I sense you're the kind of person that …"*
(speak about what you sense they are they like and/or what are they good at)

➢ *"I can see God using you to…."* or
"I believe something God wants to do in your life is…"

➢ "Can I share something with you that'll make you smile?" (especially w/ strangers)

➢ Speak in faith and love.

➢ Get feedback by saying "Did that ring true to you?"

As you are growing, give yourself permission to "step out on a limb" by using phrases like, "I might be wrong, but I sense God wants you to know…" Get immediate feedback. "Does that make sense?" You'll learn as you go, whether you're "off" or "right on".

III. LOOK UP
PRACTICE
1. a. Get into groups of 3 or 4. You will take turns receiving words from the others. Go from the shortest person in the group to the tallest receiving words of encouragement from the others.

Each of those who are NOT the one receiving the words of encouragement, will take turns speaking. Go through the following exercises. Keep the Words brief and encouraging. Keep your eyes open and keep it conversational. When one person stops, the next one should start quickly. Don't wait. Speak God's truth! (No "waiting on a word from God." Open your mouth and God will fill it.)

Go through the following exercises in rounds in the group. Ask the Lord a specific question about the people in your group, then share a word of encouragement from what He shows you.

Do one question each round:
- One of the ways I see Jesus at work in you is…? I could see God using you to…

- What super hero or movie character do they remind you of? Why?

- What Bible character are they like? Why?

- What Bible verse do you have for them? Why?

b. Give one another feedback.
- When did you feel most stretched by the Holy Spirit as you were speaking?

- When did you feel particularly encouraged or like God was speaking to you through someone in the group?

PLAN
1. Learn to incorporate prophesy with prayer.
a. Select a friend and pray for them. Ask God to give you specific insight into His heart for them and pray these blessings into their lives.

b. Call your friend and share what God put in your heart for them. Encourage them. Then ask them if anything you shared connected with anything in particular they've been going through.

2. Begin to develop a vision for a lifestyle of prophetic encouragement.

Purpose to speak prophetic words of encouragement to people as a lifestyle. This week, in private begin to practice approaching people in an imaginary scenario. Envision common scenarios such as speaking to a cashiers, table waiters, random persons at the mall that draw your attention, etc. Get comfortable opening the conversation and opening the door to speak into their lives.

PRAY
If anyone needs healing or prayer, lay hands and minister to one another.

CHAPTER 10
BAPTIZING BELIEVERS
IN THE HOLY SPIRIT

I. LOOK BACK-

A. How have you experienced **God at work *in you*** this past week? Share any highlights, lessons, insights or encouragement.

B. How have you experienced **God at work *through you*** to touch others this past week? How did your assignment to pray prophetically over a friend and then share with them what God showed you? What did you experience? Share any highlights or challenges.

II. LESSON

It is no coincidence that Jesus Christ used the same word "baptism" to refer to baptism in water and in the Holy Spirit. God wants our lives to become a demonstration of His Kingdom as we are immersed into Him.

In this lesson we will learn about the importance of the Baptism of the Holy Spirit, its relationship with speaking in other tongues, and how to minister to others so that they can receive the Baptism of the Holy Spirit.

BAPTISM IN THE HOLY SPIRIT
1) In the Scriptures below
a. UNDERLINE every phrase that indicates WHO is baptized in the Holy Spirit.
b. CIRCLE every phrase that indicates the results of being baptized in the Holy Spirit.
c. ANSWER the questions following each of

Video 10.1 (15 min.) Ministering the Baptism of the Holy Spirit

the verses below based on the verse(s) immediately above the question.

On the last day of the feast, the great day, Jesus stood up and cried out, "If anyone thirsts, let him come to me and drink. Whoever believes in me, as the Scripture has said, 'Out of his inmost being (lit. belly) will flow rivers of living water.'" Now this he said about the Spirit, whom those who believed in him were to receive, for as yet the Spirit had not been given, because Jesus was not yet glorified. Joh 7:36-39

What does God say the Spirit will do?

Where does He flow out from— our brain or our belly? Why is this important?

And divided tongues as of fire appeared to them and rested on each one of them. And they were all filled with the Holy Spirit and began to speak in other tongues as the Spirit gave them utterance... And Peter said to them, "Repent and be baptized every one of you in the name of Jesus Christ for the forgiveness of your sins, and you will receive the gift of the Holy Spirit. For the promise is for you and for your children and for all who are far off, everyone whom the Lord our God calls to himself." Acts 2:3-4, 38-40

What is the relationship between being filled with the Holy Spirit and speaking in other tongues at the initial experience of the Baptism of the Holy Spirit on Pentecost?

Who spoke in tongues?

Who supplied the utterance?

"in one Spirit we were all baptized into one body—Jews or Greeks, slaves or free—and all were made to drink of one Spirit." 1 Cor. 12:12-13

But when they believed Philip as he preached good news about the Kingdom of God and the name of Jesus Christ, they were baptized, both men and women... Now when the apostles at Jerusalem heard that Samaria had received the Word of God, they sent to them Peter and John, who came down and prayed for them that they might receive the Holy Spirit, for he had not yet fallen on any of them, but they had only been baptized in the name of the Lord Jesus. Then they laid their hands on them and they received the Holy Spirit. Act 8:12-17

Did the apostles view the baptism of the Holy Spirit as a imperceptible experience that should be received by faith, or a real experience of God's Spirit with observable demonstration?

What did the apostles do to help these new believers experience the baptism of the Holy Spirit?

So Ananias (NOT an apostle) *departed and entered the house. And laying his hands on him he said, "Brother Saul, the Lord Jesus who appeared to you on the road by which you came has sent me so that you may regain your sight and be filled with the Holy Spirit." Act 9:17*

Do you need to have a special office in the church to minister in the power of the Holy Spirit?

What did he do to help Paul be filled with the Holy Spirit?

And it happened that while Apollos was at Corinth, Paul passed through the inland country and came to Ephesus. There he found some disciples. And he said to them, "Did you receive the Holy Spirit when you believed?" And they said, "No, we have not even heard that there is a Holy Spirit." And he said, "Into what then were you baptized?" They said, "Into John's baptism." And Paul said, "John baptized with the baptism of repentance, telling the people to believe in the one who was to come after him, that is, Jesus." On hearing this, they were baptized in the name of the Lord Jesus. And when Paul had laid his hands on them, the Holy Spirit came on them, and they began speaking in tongues and prophesying. Act 19:1-6

How did Paul go about discerning whether someone was a true disciple of Jesus Christ?

How did Paul minister to help people receive the baptism of the Holy Spirit?

What was the evidence that people had received the baptism of the Holy Spirit?

For this reason I remind you to fan into flame the gift of God, which is in you through the laying on of my hands, for God gave us a spirit not of fear but of power and love and self-control. 2 Tim. 1:6-7

SPEAKING IN TONGUES

Because of the close relationship between baptism in the Holy Spirit and speaking in heavenly tongues, it's important to understand the place of speaking in new tongues in the life of a believer in Christ.

1) In the Scriptures below

a. UNDERLINE every phrase that indicates WHO God says CAN speak in tongues.

b. CIRCLE every phrase that indicates the benefits of speaking in tongues

c. ANSWER the questions following each of the verses below based on the verse(s) immediately above the question.

And he said to them, "Go into all the world and proclaim the gospel to the whole creation. Whoever believes and is baptized will be saved, but whoever does not believe will be condemned. And these signs will accompany those who believe: in my name they will cast out demons; they will speak in new tongues…" Mark 16:15-18

Who did Jesus say will speak in new tongues?

Now I want you all to speak in tongues, but even more to prophesy. 1 Cor.14:5

What was Paul's attitude to speaking in tongues?

I thank God that I speak in tongues more than all of you. 1 Cor.14:18

What was Paul's practice regarding speaking in tongues?

Pursue love, and earnestly desire the spiritual gifts… 1 Cor.14:1

Did Paul teach that we are limited in the gifts in which we can operate? Or that we should pursue activating every gift we desire to build up the body of Christ?

Now there are varieties of gifts, but the same Spirit; and there are varieties of service, but the same Lord; and there are varieties of activities, but it is the same God who empowers them all in everyone. 1 Cor.12:4-6

Although there is a great variety of expression of the gifts, how many gifts does God empower?

In whom?

And he said to them, "Did you receive the Holy Spirit when you believed?" And they said, "No, we have not even heard that there is a Holy Spirit." And he said, "Into what then were you baptized?" They said, "Into John's baptism." And Paul said, "John baptized with the baptism of repentance, telling the people to believe in the one who was to come after him, that is, Jesus." On hearing this, they were baptized in the name of the Lord Jesus. And when Paul had laid his hands on them, the Holy Spirit came on them, and they began speaking in tongues and prophesying. Act 19:2-6

What place did the Baptism of the Holy Spirit and speaking in tongues play in the ministry of the apostle Paul?

Paul writes, *"indeed, God set **in the assembly**, first apostles, secondly prophets, thirdly teachers, afterwards powers, afterwards gifts of healings, helpings, governings, divers kinds of tongues; are all apostles? are all prophets? are all teachers? are all powers? have all gifts of healings? do all speak with tongues? do all interpret?"* 1 Cor. 12:28-39

Did Paul teach that some people CAN'T ever speak in tongues? Or that not everyone speaks in tongues during an assembly of the body?

"The one who speaks in a tongue builds up himself" 1 Cor. 14:4

Even though tongues does not build up the church directly, could there be an *indirect benefit to the body of Christ* as a result of someone speaking in tongues to build themselves up? Explain.

"For one who speaks in a tongue speaks not to men but to God; for no one understands him, but he utters mysteries in the Spirit" 1 Cor. 14:2

Who is speaking when a believer speaks in tongues? What is He speaking? What is the spiritual significance of this?

Who understands him?

(This indicates that tongues was NOT always a known human language as on the day of Pentecost.)

If any speak in a tongue, *let there be only two or at most three, and **each in turn**, and let someone interpret. But if there is no one to interpret, let each of them **keep silent** in church and **speak to himself and to God**.* 1 Cor. 14:27-28

Based on these instructions, does Paul believe that Christians have the ability to determine when and where they will speak in tongues? Why is this significant?

And they were all filled with the Holy Spirit and began to speak in other tongues as the Spirit gave them utterance. Acts 2:4

Categorize various activities from the preceding verse— which one(s) does God do? Which activities do we do in cooperation with what God is doing?

 - filled with the Holy Spirit: God or us?

- speak in other tongues: God or us?

- Spirit gave them utterance: God or us?

KEY LESSONS:

- The baptism of the Holy Spirit is always perceptible experience of God's Spirit pouring out through the believer in a heavenly prayer language and/or prophetic praise.

- Believers have the privilege of ministering the baptism of the Holy Spirit to others by laying on of hands.

- Ask people about their experience of the Holy Spirit. We should follow the example of apostles and ask people who claim to be believers in Jesus Christ about their experience of the Holy Spirit (not to judge them, but to see where we may be able to help them).

III. LOOK OUT:
PRACTICE
1. Discussion: For those who have already experience the baptism of the Holy Spirit-

How did you first experience the baptism of the Holy Spirit?

What barriers did you have to cross to receive the baptism of the Holy Spirit and how did God help you cross those barriers?

2. How to lay hands on people for the baptism of the Holy Spirit.

In order to minister the baptism of the Holy Spirit, help people receive the outflowing of the Holy Spirit and activate their own heavenly prayer language. Here's what I say and do:

"Jesus died to give you the Holy Spirit, not just to live in you, but to flow out through you in a supernatural way. Jesus said the operation of the Holy Spirit is like "rivers of living water flowing out of our belly, or inmost being." As this river begins to flow out from you, it will start by God giving you the gift of a heavenly prayer language just like it says in Acts 2:4 "they were all filled with the Holy Spirit and began to speak in other tongues as the Spirit gave them utterance." I'm going to lay hands on you. I believe you will begin to experience God's presence filling you. Just receive His presence. Then allow His presence to begin to bubble up through your voice. As you sense His presence rising up within you, just take a step of faith and begin to speak syllables you don't understand, and God will supply to you a divine utterance that is flowing out from His Spirit, not your mind."

Then have them put their hands on their own belly. You can place your hands on theirs. Then lead them in a prayer asking God for the baptism of the Holy Spirit and their own heavenly prayer language. Then begin to release the power of God by faith and pray in your own heavenly prayer language. Allow them to experience God's presence filling them. Many begin to speak in tongues spontaneously at this point. However, some believers may need some encouragement to help them to release themselves to speak out their new language, but don't put any pressure on people. Simply help people by removing any barriers people hang on to that are holding back God's free flow within them.

3. Practice Praying in Tongues as a group. Everyone stand up and hold hands. Anyone who does not yet speak in tongues can begin to pray in tongues during this exercise. Speak in tongues fervently for 2 minutes. Then Speak in tongues softly for 1 minute. The Speak in tongues fervently for 2 minutes.

(BTW- This does NOT violate instructions regarding tongues in the public assembly of the church, because everyone is instructed about tongues and there is not the possibility of anyone being confused.)

4. Hands On- Find out if there is anyone in the group that has not yet experienced the Baptism of the Holy Spirit. If anyone still needs the Baptism of the Holy Spirit, lay hands on them and minister the Baptism of the Holy Spirit.

PLAN

1. Many times people are experiencing the benefits of praying in their heavenly prayer language but never associate the accelerated changes with praying in their heavenly prayer language. This week, implement a practice of speaking in tongues for at least 30 minutes each day for one week (3x 10 min. or 2 x 15 min. or 10 x 3 min.). Make a note of spiritual changes you experience this week. What is your plan?

2. Who do you know that may not yet be baptized in Holy Spirit? You can ask, teach, and minister to them. Write their name and when you will talk with them.

PRAY

a. Pray for laborers to be sent out into the Harvest.

b. If anyone needs healing or prayer, lay hands and minister to one another.

CHAPTER 11
SPEAKING SUPERNATURAL
WORDS OF ENCOURAGEMENT
AND DIVINE INSIGHT (PART 2)

I. LOOK BACK-

A. How have you experienced **God at work *in you*** this past week? Share your experience from praying in tongues 30 minutes each day— highlights, lessons, insights or encouragement.

B. How have you experienced **God at work *through you*** to touch others this past week? How did your assignment to talk about the baptism of the Holy Spirit with a friend go? What did you experience? Share any highlights or challenges.

II. LESSON

In this lesson we will learn the importance of speaking according to God's created value, redemptive work, and eternal destiny for each person. Although God can reveal particular details about individuals, as believers, we have heard what God says about every person. We must learn to express God's heart spontaneously.

1) Read the passage below

a. UNDERLINE those phrases that reveal God's value and destiny for people.

b. ANSWER any questions based on the preceding verse.

But no human being can tame the tongue. It is a restless evil, full of deadly poison. With it we bless our Lord and Father, and with it we curse people who are made in the likeness of God. From the same mouth come blessing and cursing. My brothers, these things ought not to be so. James 3:8-10

From this passage, what is the basis for God's value for each person ?

How might you express a blessing for someone based on the fact that God created them in His likeness and maintains that original value for them?

Jesus, the mediator of a new covenant, and to the sprinkled blood that speaks a better word than the blood of Abel. Heb 12:24

What does the blood of Jesus Christ say about people and about God?

For while we were still powerless, at the right time Christ died for the ungodly… but God shows his love for us in that while we were still sinners, Christ died for us. Rom 5:6,8

What does the death of Christ say for those who are powerless, ungodly, and still sinners?

How does that differ from what the church is typically saying for powerless, ungodly sinners?

He died for all, that those who live might no longer live for themselves but for him who for their sake died and was raised. From now on, therefore, we regard no one according to the flesh. Even though we once regarded Christ according to the flesh, we regard him thus no longer. 2Co 5:15-19

What does the cross and resurrection say about how God regards people?

And being made perfect, Jesus became the author of eternal salvation unto all them that obey him Heb 5:9

What has Jesus Christ written for every person? What does His book say about what He can do for every life?

Look back at your answers to the questions above. What would happen if you began speaking these things spontaneously into the lives of the people you meet every day?

MASTER DEMONSTRATION

Jesus demonstrated how He spoke prophetically in His personal ministry on many occasions. Take, for example, Jesus' encounter with the woman at the well.

1) Read the passage below,
a. UNDERLINE those phrases in which Jesus revealed God's value and destiny for this lady
b. CIRCLE those phrases in which Jesus revealed who He is and what He can do for this lady
c. SHADE those phrases in which Jesus revealed God's personal knowledge of this lady

Jn. 4:6-29 Jacob's well was there; so Jesus, wearied as he was from his journey, was sitting beside the well. It was about the sixth hour. A woman from Samaria came to draw water. Jesus said to her, "***Give me a drink***." (For his disciples had gone away into the city to buy food.) The Samaritan woman said to him, "How is it that you, a Jew, ask for a drink from me, a woman of Samaria?" (For Jews have no dealings with Samaritans.) Jesus answered her, "If you knew ***the gift of God***, and who it is that is saying to you, 'Give me a drink,' you would have asked him, and he would have given you ***living water***." The woman said to him, "Sir, you have nothing to draw water with, and the well is deep. Where do you get that living water? Are you greater than our father Jacob? He gave us the well and drank from it himself, as did his sons and his livestock." Jesus said to her, "***Everyone who drinks of this water will be thirsty again, but whoever drinks of the water that I will give him will never be thirsty again. The water that I will give him will become in him a spring of water welling up to eternal life.***" The woman said to him, "Sir, give me this water, so that I will not be thirsty or have to come here to draw water." Jesus said to her, **"Go, call your husband, and come here**." The woman answered him, "I have no husband." Jesus said to her, **"You are right in saying, 'I have no husband'; for you have had five husbands, and the one you now have is not your husband. What you have said is true**." The woman said to him, "Sir, I perceive that you are a prophet. Our fathers worshiped on this mountain, but you say that in Jerusalem is the place where people ought to worship." Jesus said to her, **"Woman, believe me, the hour is coming when neither on this mountain nor in Jerusalem will you worship the Father**. You worship what you do not know; we worship what we know, for salvation is from the Jews. But **the hour is coming, and is now here, when the true worshipers will worship the Father in spirit and truth, for the Father is seeking such people to worship him. God is spirit, and those who worship him must worship in spirit and truth**." The woman said to him, "I know that Messiah is coming (he who is called Christ). When he comes, he will tell us all things." Jesus said to her, **"I who speak to you am he."** Just then his disciples came back. They marveled that he was talking with a woman, but no one said, "What do you seek?" or, "Why are you talking with her?" So the woman left her water jar and went away into town and said to the people, "Come, see a man who told me all that I ever did. Can this be the Christ?"

How does Jesus speaking accomplish "up building and encouragement and consolation" (1 Cor. 14:3)?

In what ways did Jesus speak into this lady's life to reveal God's value, destiny, and salvation?

What are some of the things Jesus did to start the conversation and to move it forward?

What might have happened if Jesus, instead of asking for a drink, tried to start the conversation, "You've had five husbands, and you're living with a man who isn't your husband now?"

What can we learn from the way Jesus approached unbelievers?

How did Jesus' interaction with the woman at the well demonstrate the following principles?:

➢ Make strangers your friends by breaking barriers in love to connect with them. Speak to them and be their friend.

➢ Create curiosity about spiritual things. Stir up desire for spiritual things.

➢ Use common, non-religious language that people understand to speak about spiritual realities that people don't understand.

➢ Use the natural objects and activities to reveal God's invisible, eternal, and supernatural realities.

➢ God speaks to reveal our value, remove our bondages and to restore us to His destiny. When God reveals sin, it's spoken in a way to elevate us to our true destiny.

➢ Our desires are intended to lead us to God. God corrects destructive direction, not God given desires. Sin is what people do when they allow God given desires to go astray. The prophet points the heart back to God.

III. LOOK UP

PRACTICE
1. Speaking from Object Association Exercise
Just as Jesus spoke a Word based on the natural activity of the woman drawing water from the well, often God will start with natural objects or actions to unleash His Word into someone's life.

For example:
As Samuel turned to go away, Saul seized the skirt of his robe, and it tore. And Samuel said to him, "The LORD has torn the kingdom of Israel from you this day and has given it to a neighbor of yours, who is better than you. 1Sa 15:27-28

The word of the LORD came to me a second time, saying, "What do you see?" And I said, "I see a boiling pot, facing away from the north." Then the LORD said to me, "Out of the north disaster shall be let loose upon all the inhabitants of the land. Jer 1:13-14

a. Divide the group in half. Send half the group out of the room.

b. Those that are left in the room should gather random objects and lay them out on a table or chair. Have the group that is out of the room come back in. Give them the following instructions. "Please select one of the objects that are laid out on the table. Once you've selected it. Hold it in front of you so we can see what you chose."

c. Let the people in the room observe the people and the objects they chose. Each one without an object speaks spontaneous words of encouragement over those who are holding objects based on the objects they chose.

d. Switch roles. Send the group that stayed out of the room. Switch objects. Gather new objects. Repeat the exercise.

e. Give one another feedback.

- When did you feel most stretched by the Holy Spirit as you were speaking?

- When did you feel particularly encouraged or like God was speaking to you through someone in the group?

PLAN

1. Begin to develop a lifestyle of speaking LIFE. Purpose to speak into the lives of 3 strangers this week. Be sure to invite their feedback. "Did any of that make sense to you or seem to fit what's going on in your life right now?" You'll be sharing about these encounters next week.

2. Continue to pray regularly, "Jesus, help me to see people through your eyes so that you can touch them through my life."

PRAY

If anyone needs healing or prayer, lay hands and minister to one another.

CHAPTER 12
SPEAKING SUPERNATURAL
WORDS OF ENCOURAGEMENT
AND DIVINE INSIGHT (PART 3)

I. LOOK BACK-
A. How have you experienced **God at work *in you*** this past week? Share any highlights, lessons, insights or encouragement.

B. How have you experienced **God at work *through you*** to touch others this past week? How did your assignment to speak prophetically into the lives of 3 strangers go? What did you experience? Share any highlights or challenges.

II. LESSON
God wants to speak very personally into people's lives through you. It's one of the ways He reveals Himself today. Because Jesus Christ lives in you, He can speak through you into the lives of others in very powerful ways.

There is a great deal of variety in how God will speak to and through His people. In this lesson we will learn different ways in which God speaks and how to discern God's Spirit from deceitful spirits.

1) Read the verses below.
a. UNDERLINE every phrase that indicates a WAY IN WHICH GOD can speak through us
b. CIRCLE those phrases that indicate variables that influence how God speaks through us.

And in the last days it shall be, God declares, that I will pour out my Spirit on all flesh, and your sons and your daughters shall prophesy, and your young men shall see visions, and your old men shall dream dreams; even on my male servants and female servants in those days I will pour out my Spirit, and they shall prophesy. Act 2:17-18

To each is given the manifestation of the Spirit for the common good. For to one is given through the Spirit the word of wisdom, and to another the word of knowledge according to the same Spirit … to another prophecy, to another the ability to distinguish between spirits, to another various kinds of tongues, to another the interpretation of tongues. All these are empowered by one and the same Spirit, who apportions to each one individually as he wills. 1Co 12:7-11

Pursue love, and earnestly desire the spiritual gifts, especially that you may prophesy. 1 Cor. 14:1

And the scribes and the Pharisees watched him, to see whether he would heal on the Sabbath, so that they might find a reason to accuse him. But he knew their thoughts… Luke 6:7-8

Having gifts that differ… let us use them: if prophecy, in proportion to our faith… Rom 12:6

Let no corrupting talk come out of your mouths, but only such as is good for building up, as fits the occasion, that it may give grace to those who hear. Eph 4:29

Let your speech always be gracious, seasoned with salt, so that you may know how you ought to answer each person. Col 4:6

Based on the preceding passages, what are some of the variety of ways God can speak to and through us?

What are some variables that influence the way God speaks through us?

Common ways the Spirit of God can communicate with us:
- ✓ You See something… either in an open vision or in our imagination. God brings a picture to mind or before us.
- ✓ You Feel something… a pain or sensation in our body as a signal or "sympathy pain" for someone in your proximity
- ✓ You Hear something… a thought that comes spontaneously (like God "sent us a private message" that pops into our head) or audibly
- ✓ You Know something… you just know.
- ✓ You Sense something… a holy hunch, sanctified intuition.
- ✓ You Dream something… something you dream is connected to the events of your life
- ✓ You Remember something… the Holy Spirit brings a particular Scripture or event to mind.

In which of the above ways have you already experienced God speaking to you? What ways are most common for you?

STAYING ON TRACK WITH GOD

It's possible for those who believe in God's ability to communicate with us alongside of the Bible to get off track, off center, and confused because they neglect the Scriptures and following Jesus Christ as His disciple-making disciple.

2) Read the passages below

a. **UNDERLINE** every phrase that indicates something GOD DOES to help us stay on track with Him.

b. **CIRCLE** every phrase that indicates something that WE DO to stay on track with God.

c. **SHADE** every phrase that indicates something that WE should AVOID to steer clear of deception.

When the Spirit of truth comes, he will guide you into all the truth, for he will not speak on his own authority, but whatever he hears he will speak, and he will declare to you the things that are to come. He will glorify me, for he will take what is mine and declare it to you. John 16:13-14

Sanctify them in the truth; your word is truth. John 17:17

Beloved, do not believe every spirit, but test the spirits to see whether they are from God, for many false prophets have gone out into the world. By this you know the Spirit of God: every spirit that confesses that Jesus Christ has come in the flesh is from God, and every spirit that does not confess Jesus is not from God. This is the spirit of the antichrist, which you heard was coming and now is in the world already. Little children, you are from God and have overcome them, for he who is in you is greater than he who is in the world. They are from the world; therefore they speak from the world, and the world listens to them. We are from God. Whoever knows God listens to us; whoever is not from God does not listen to us. By this we know the Spirit of truth and the spirit of error. 1Jn 4:1-6

I am a fellow servant with you and your brothers who hold to the testimony of Jesus. Worship God." For the testimony of Jesus is the spirit of prophecy. Rev 19:10

Based on the Scriptures above, what would you say is a clear indication someone is speaking from God?

Based on the Scriptures above, what would you say is a clear indication someone is NOT speaking from God?

GUIDING PRINCIPLES:

➤ The Holy Spirit glorifies Jesus Christ and builds us up into His image.

➤ The testimony of Jesus Christ is the Spirit of Prophesy. When we prophesy, we speak in agreement with the revelation of what God revealed when the Word was made flesh and walked among us by the power of the Holy Spirit.

➤ The Spirit of God speaks consistently with the written Word and obedience to Jesus Christ.

➤ We must test every spirit. Yet we don't walk in fear, because God lives in us.

➤ We have all the revelation we need in Jesus Christ. The Spirit of prophesy helps us to proclaim this revelation spontaneously and powerfully.

Can you share an example of ways you've seen these principles from the Word ignored in personal ministry? What were the consequences?

How can we help one another hear God and NOT get off track?

III. LOOK FORWARD:
PRACTICE
1. GROUP EXERCISE: "Flying By Your Instruments"

a). **Divide the group in half**. Have half of the group stand up, spread out, and close their eyes. Silently, the others move to stand in front of someone who has their eyes closed and place one finger on their shoulder to let them know that someone is in front of them.

Those who have their eyes closed are going to speak a prophetic word for the person in front of them WITHOUT OPENING THEIR EYES. They are encouraged to ask God questions and speak words of encouragement and insight according to whatever God brings to mind. After they are done, have them open their eyes.

b) **Give feedback.**

c) **Switch roles and repeat the exercise.**

2. Role Play.

a) Partner up. Practice approaching strangers to share a prophetic word of encouragement. Act out the following scenarios:

- Prophetic word to grocery store Cashier as you are checking out

- Prophetic word to a table server as they take your order

- Prophetic word to a stranger in a dentist lobby

- Prophetic word to a fellow shopper at the mall or store

b) Switch roles and repeat the exercises.

PLAN

1. Continue to develop a lifestyle of speaking LIFE. Purpose to speak into the lives of at least 3 strangers this week. Be sure to invite their feedback. "Did any of that make sense to you or seem to fit what's going on in your life right now?" You'll be sharing about these encounters next week.

2. Continue to pray regularly, "Jesus, help me to see people through your eyes so that you can touch them through my life."

PRAY
If anyone needs healing or prayer, lay hands and minister to one another.

CHAPTER 13
LAUNCHING NEW MOVES OF GOD

I. LOOK BACK-
A. How have you experienced **God at work** *in you* this past week? Share any highlights, lessons, insights or encouragement.

B. How have you experienced **God at work** *through you* to touch others this past week? How did your assignment to minister healing to your friends and some store employees go? What did you experience? Share any highlights or challenges.

II. LESSON
In this lesson you will learn the practices and patterns that Jesus Christ and the apostles used to launch new moves of God.

Jesus Christ and the apostles were not attached to buildings or organizations. They advanced the Kingdom of God into new people groups by making themselves available to key people people who were receptive to them and their ministry by getting involved *on their turf to help them reach the people in their circle of influence.*

> **Video 13.2**
> **(5 min.)**
>
> **Infiltrate. Don't Extract.**

1) In the Scriptures below
a. UNDERLINE every phrase that indicates God's vision to launch new moves of the Kingdom among a group of people, not merely to win individual souls and extract them out of the world to build a congregation.
b. CIRCLE every reference to a place or food.
c. ANSWER the questions following each of the verses below based on the verse(s) immediately above the question.

When the jailer woke and ... called for lights and rushed in, and trembling with fear he fell down before Paul and Silas. Then he brought them out and said, "Sirs, what must I do to be saved?" And they said, "Believe in the Lord Jesus, and you will be saved, you and your household." And they spoke the word of the Lord to him and to all who were in his house. And he took them the same hour of the night and washed their wounds; and he was baptized at once, he and all his family. Then he brought them up into his house and set food before them. And he rejoiced along with his entire household that he had believed in God. Acts 16:27-34

If Paul had not understood God's pattern of winning not just the individual, but the entire circle of influence, what would have been the result?

For the jailer?

For his family?

For his extended house hold (circle of influence)?

How would that effect the overall impact for the kingdom in this region?

God wants to reap vineyards, not just pluck a grape.

How do we see the following Kingdom tactics at work in this passage?

> **Video 13.3**
> **(9 min.)**
>
> **The Practice of Reaching Groups vs. Individuals**

- One of the ways you can reach your circle of influence is by connecting strong Christians with the people in your circle on THEIR TURF.

- Whenever your reach one person, instead of bringing them into an existing group, look for ways to get involved in their life and help them reach their Circle of Influence to start a new group.

- Be a connector. Win Circles, not just individuals. Start new Groups.

- Today's person of peace is tomorrow's laborer in the harvest.

What mindsets and practices will we need to change to adopt these practices today?

The two disciples heard him say this, and they followed Jesus. Jesus turned and saw them following and said to them, "What are you seeking?" And they said to him, "Rabbi" (which means Teacher), "where are you staying?" He said to them, "Come and you will see." So they came and saw where he was staying, and they stayed with him that day, for it was about the tenth hour. John 1"37-39

One of the two who heard John speak and followed Jesus was Andrew, Simon Peter's brother. He first found his own brother Simon and said to him, "We have found the Messiah" (which means Christ). He brought him to Jesus. Jesus looked at him and said, "You are Simon the son of John. You shall be called Cephas" (which means Peter). John 1:40-42

And when Jesus entered Peter's house, he saw his mother-in-law lying sick with a fever. he saw his mother-in-law lying sick with a fever. He touched her hand, and the fever left her, and she rose and began to serve him. That evening they brought to him many who were oppressed by demons, and he cast out the spirits with a word and healed all who were sick. Matt. 8:14-16

Trace the string of relationships that Jesus followed on the way towards launching a move of God in a new region. Write their names below.

Instead of extracting individuals "out of the wild" to invite them to the "zoo" where they can "be fed" by their favorite "zoo keeper", whenever possible, they started new works by connecting with new believers on their turf to bring the Kingdom of God to their entire circle of pre-existing relationships to impact this region. They didn't extract. They infiltrated. Jesus and the apostles never forgot how to live in the wild. They didn't live in captivity or build zoos or need zookeepers to feed the saints and keep them alive. They raised up warriors to exercise the dominion of the Kingdom of God in fellowship together.

**Video 13.1
(10 min.)**

Jesus Models how to Advance the Kingdom

2) In the Scriptures below

a. UNDERLINE every phrase that indicates something that the disciples are to do to launch a new move of the Kingdom.

b. CIRCLE every phrase that indicates something that the "Person of Peace" does.

c. ANSWER the questions following each of the verses below based on the verse(s) immediately above the question.

After this the Lord appointed seventy-two others and sent them on ahead of him, two by two, into every town and place where he himself was about to go. And he said to them, "The harvest is plentiful, but the laborers are few. Therefore pray earnestly to the Lord of the harvest to send out laborers into his harvest.

*Go your way; behold, I am sending you out as lambs in the midst of wolves. Carry no moneybag, no knapsack, no sandals, and greet no one on the road. Whatever house you enter, first say, 'Peace be to this house!' And if a **person of peace** is there, your peace will rest upon him. But if not, it will return to you. And remain in the same house, eating and drinking what they provide, for the laborer deserves his wages. Do not go from house to house. Whenever you enter a town and they receive you, eat what is set before you. Heal the sick in it and say to them, 'The kingdom of God has come near to you.'*

But whenever you enter a town and they do not receive you, go into its streets and say, 'Even the dust of your town that clings to our feet we wipe off against you. Nevertheless know this, that the kingdom of God has come near.' Luke 10:1-11

List the things that the disciples do to launch new moves of God:

List the things that the person of peace does as part of this process:

A person of peace will exhibit 3 characteristics.

1. They are receptive to YOU.

2. They are receptive to YOUR MINISTRY.

3. They are willing to connect you with their circle of influence.

The person of peace is the doorway to a new circle of influence. Once you find a person of peace, you are no longer a stranger. You become the honored guest of a trusted friend. Our ministry to strangers is part of the process to find a person of peace.

*And whatever town or village you enter, **enquire** who is worthy in it and stay there until you depart.* Matt.10:11

> **Video 13.4**
> **(10 min.)**
>
> **Launching New Moves of God by Understanding Persons of Peace**

In western cultures, when people are receptive to you and your ministry, they will often ask you things like, "Where do you go to church?" Often, what they are *really* asking is, "How can I get what you have?"

Here are two simple questions that can be used to identify a person of peace as you interact with people who have experienced your ministry to see if they are a "Person of Peace"

The "Person of Peace" Questions:

1) **Would you be interested in meeting in your home to learn more about how you can experience God in your daily life from the Bible?**

2) **Who else do you know that might need this?**

SUMMARY:

God wants to reach entire circles of influence, not merely individuals. God wants to use each of us to reach our circle of influence, and also to launch new moves of the Kingdom. As we minister to strangers, some will be receptive to us and to our ministry. These are "persons of peace". As we make ourselves available to get involved in their lives on their turf to help bring the Kingdom of God to their circle of influence, new works of God are unleashed and new workers are equipped.

III. LOOK OUT:
PRACTICE

1. In your group, take a few minutes to do the following:

A. Individually identify the people in your circle of influence. Your circle of influence consists of the people with whom you share family news and would be influenced by your recommendations. Write their names in the space below.

B. Now, circle the names of the 3-5 people you believe that the Holy Spirit wants you to make your REACH priority. Begin praying for them daily and making opportunities to share your story and minister the Kingdom to them.

2. Get a partner and role play.

a. Practice asking the person of peace questions to one another until you are both comfortable asking these questions and have them memorized.

b. Practice putting it all together. Role play spontaneous ministry to a stranger in a public place. You can share your testimony, speak a spontaneous word of blessing, and/or minister healing in whatever order seems most natural. At the end of the scenario, practice asking the person of peace question at the conclusion of a ministry scenario.

c. Change roles. Repeat the exercise until you are both confident and comfortable.

PLAN

1. Incorporate the activities that are going to enable you to find a person of peace and be part of launching a new move of God in your city. What are your goals? How much time will you reserve each week to minister to strangers until you find a person of peace?

2. Once you find a person of peace, the time that you've been spending to reach strangers can be used to work with a person of peace to reach their circle of influence.

3. Make a plan to start a new group by using the *Immersed into God Interactive Training Manual.* All you need to do is to find one or two people you can help. If you need to, you can partner up with someone in your group and combine your efforts to start a new group. What's your plan?

PRAY

a. Pray for laborers to be sent out into the Harvest.

b. If anyone needs healing or prayer, lay hands and minister to one another.

CHAPTER 14
PROCLAIMING THE KING AND THE KINGDOM

I. LOOK BACK-

A. Let's share our goals and plans to find a person of peace and start new groups. What are your plans? What did you do this week?

B. How can we encourage, support and partner together to multiply new groups?

II. LESSON

This lesson will equip you to be able to lead people to Jesus Christ by sharing the gospel in a simple way called the "God Container Story"

A. Read the main points of the "God Container" Story out loud together several times.

GOD CONTAINER STORY:

- **God created us to contain Him and be filled with His Spirit so that people would be God's representatives on earth.**

- **We closed our hearts to God. We became empty and alienated from God, filled with all kinds of lies and pain.**

- **God sent Jesus Christ to save us and restore us to God's original purpose.**

   A. Jesus Christ showed us who God is.
   He is God in the flesh, living through a man. He showed us that God wants to heal us, to forgive us, to break the power of evil over our lives, and to bring us to live with Him forever.

   B. Jesus Christ showed us God's purpose for man.
   God created us to be filled with His presence, just like Jesus. Jesus lived for us, and died on the cross for our sins, and rose from the dead to break the power of death and evil. He did all this so that He could give us the Spirit of God that lived in Him.

- **When we surrender our lives to Jesus Christ, He forgives us and gives us the gift of the Holy Spirit.**

This is why Jesus told people who come to Him to be baptized, which is a picture of burying our old self under the water, being cleansed from our sins, and being completely immersed into Jesus Christ and the power of God's Spirit. God buries the old you with all its junk and makes you a brand new person. He comes to live inside you by the presence of the Holy Spirit. Would you like to receive Jesus Christ and become His follower so that you can be forgiven and filled with God?

TWO ILLUSTRATIONS

One way to make the "God Container" story understandable is to use examples and illustrations from everyday life. Two examples that I use repeatedly when sharing Jesus Christ with others are water bottles (for the summer) and gloves (for the winter). I share these illustrations below for you to use as you see fit. Read the examples below out loud and answer the discussion questions below.

Water Bottles

Just like an empty water bottle is easier to crush than one that is filled, the reasons our lives are so messed up is because we are empty. God created us to contain His love, truth and power. But we walked away from God and became filled with lies, insecurity, fear, and a bunch of other things that we were never meant to have inside of us. This is what made Jesus Christ different. The creator of the universe humbled Himself to join the human race and live as a man, but man as He originally intended— a man filled with the Spirit of God. Jesus Christ contained God. He loved perfectly, and spoke the truth with wisdom beyond this world. He even healed the sick, cast out demons, and raised the dead by releasing the power of God. Then He did something even more amazing. He died on the cross for your sins and mine so that you and I can go free and be forgiven. Then He raised from the dead after three days to demonstrate He has the power to give us eternal life. Now, if we give ourselves to Him, He pours the Spirit of God into us so that He can wash out all the junk that we're carrying around and be filled with God.

Gloves

A glove is made in the image of a hand so that it can contain a hand. We are made in the image of God so that we can contain Him. Our minds were made to contain truth and wisdom. God is perfect truth and wisdom. Our hearts were made to contain and overflow with love. God is love. But just like an empty glove doesn't hold its shape very well, we can't live the lif e we were created for without God. Without God, people can do things like lie, steal, hate, murder, use one another, and worse. God created us to be filled with His presence, so He sent Jesus Christ to rescue and restore us. Jesus Christ is the very creator of the universe who joined the human race to show us what God is like and what people were created to be— containers of God! Jesus talked often about His Father who lived within Him. It was the power and love of God that flowed out from Him that made Jesus Christ so awesome. He healed the sick, loved and forgave sinners, and exposed religious hypocrites. In Jesus Christ, we see the amazing love and power of God as He offered His life for us, so that we could go free and be forgiven, and then rose from the dead three days later! He did all this for you and I so that we could be forgiven and filled with His Spirit, just like Jesus Christ. When you give yourself to Jesus Christ, God comes into you and fills you so that He can do His works in you and through you, just like putting a hand inside of a glove.

1) **What do you like the most about the "God Container" story?**

2) **Did you notice that this is focused more on being set free from sin to be restored to live in fellowship with God and fulfill God's original purpose than merely "going to heaven when you die"? Why is this important?**

III. LOOK OUT
PRACTICE

1) As a group, take some time to worship God through the elements of the gospel. Don't allow it to be dry or routine. Mix it up and keep it real. Use the main ingredients of the gospel as "touch points" in your worship. Spend time

> **Video 14.1**
> **(14 min.)**
>
> **Overflow with the Gospel**

focusing on each one, one at a time, before moving on to the next element:
   a) Who Jesus Christ is
   b) What He accomplished
   c) The difference He makes
   d) The response He requires

2) Role play with a partner.

   a. Practice sharing the gospel using the elements of the "God container story"

Scenario: You just shared your salvation testimony and asked the question, "Do you know how Jesus Christ can do this in your life?" Your friend said, "Actually, I've always been confused by the Bible."

   b. Switch roles and allow your partner to practice their own response.

   c. Give and get feedback. What were the strong points of your response? What could make it better?

   d. Repeat the role playing exercise again and incorporate the feedback you received.

3) Role play with a partner. Developing flexibility.

   a. Share the same elements of the "God Container Story" but start in the middle or at the end, then bring the other elements into the conversation in response to the following scenario.

Scenario: You are sitting with a co-worker at the gate of the airport watching CNN as you wait for your plane. CNN reports that an arch-bishop was found to be trying to cover up several incidents of priests who were reported for abusing minors, to which your co-worker comments "It's a wonder anyone believes in God when people act like this. If God is so good, why does He let stuff like this happen when He knows it's going to turn people against Him?"

   b. Switch roles and allow your partner to practice their own response.

   c. Give and get feedback. What were the strong points of your response? What could make it better?

   d. Repeat the role playing exercise again and incorporate the feedback you received.

PLAN

1. Incorporate the elements of the "God Container" story into your personal fellowship with God so that you become comfortable expressing these truths in your own words in many different ways.

For example, "Thank you Father that you've created me to contain you..."

2. Who can you train to share the "God Container" story? Make a plan and make it happen.

3. Who do you know that may need to hear the "God Container" story? Make a plan and make it happen.

PRAY

a. Pray for laborers to be sent out into the Harvest.

b. If anyone needs healing or prayer, lay hands and minister to one another.

CHAPTER 15
BAPTIZING BELIEVERS
TO MAKE DISCIPLES

I. LOOK BACK-

A. How have you experienced **God at work *in you*** this past week? Share any highlights, lessons, insights or encouragement.

B. How have you experienced **God at work *through you*** to touch others this past week? How did your assignment go? What did you experience? Share any highlights or challenges.

II. LESSON

It is no coincidence that Jesus Christ used the same word "baptism" to refer to baptism in water and in the Holy Spirit. God wants our lives to become a demonstration of His Kingdom as we are immersed into Him.

In this lesson we will learn the significance and importance of baptizing believers in water as an act of bringing their entire body and soul into visible union with Jesus Christ.

BAPTISM IN WATER

1) In the Scriptures below

a. UNDERLINE every phrase that indicates WHO is baptized.

b. CIRCLE every phrase that indicates WHO DOES THE baptizing.

> **Video 15.1**
> **(10 min.)**
>
> **Baptizing believers**
> **to Make Disciples**

c. ANSWER the questions following each of the verses below based on the verse(s) immediately above the question.

Then Jerusalem and all Judea and all the region about the Jordan were going out to him, and they were baptized by him (John the Baptist) in the river Jordan, confessing their sins…Then Jesus came from Galilee to the Jordan to John, to be baptized by him. John would have prevented him, saying, "I need to be baptized by you, and do you come to me?" But Jesus answered him, "Let it be so now, for thus it is fitting for us to fulfill all righteousness." Then he consented. And when Jesus was baptized, immediately he went up from the water… Matt. 3:5-6,14-16

Why was Jesus baptized?

And Jesus came and said to them, "All authority in heaven and on earth has been given to me. Go therefore and make disciples of all nations, baptizing them in the name of the Father and of the Son and of the Holy Spirit, teaching them to observe all that I have commanded you. And behold, I am with you always, to the end of the age." Matt.28:18-20

Who did Jesus say should be baptized?

And he said to them, "Go into all the world and proclaim the gospel to the whole creation. Whoever believes and is baptized will be saved, but whoever does not believe will be condemned. And these signs will accompany those who believe: in my name they will cast out demons..." Mark16:15-18

What must a person do in order to be baptized?

And Peter said to them, "Repent and be baptized every one of you in the name of Jesus Christ for the forgiveness of your sins, and you will receive the gift of the Holy Spirit... So those who received his word were baptized, and there were added that day about three thousand souls. Act 2:38, 41

What does our baptism demonstrate?

So Ananias departed and entered the house. And laying his hands on him he said, "Brother Saul, the Lord Jesus who appeared to you on the road by which you came has sent me so that you may regain your sight and be filled with the Holy Spirit." And immediately something like scales fell from his eyes, and he regained his sight. Then he rose and was baptized; Act 9:17-18

Was Ananias an apostle or pastor? What does this tell us about who can baptize?

Then Philip opened his mouth, and beginning with this Scripture he told him the good news about Jesus. And as they were going along the road they came to some water, and the eunuch said, "See, here is water! What prevents me from being baptized?" And he commanded the chariot to stop, and they both went down into the water, Philip and the eunuch, and he baptized him. And when they came up out of the water, the Spirit of the Lord carried Philip away, and the eunuch saw him no more, and went on his way rejoicing. Act 8:35-38

What did the eunuch understand about the relationship between faith in Jesus Christ and baptism?

What does this tell us about baptism's place in the proclamation of the gospel?

While Peter was still saying these things, the Holy Spirit fell on all who heard the word. And the believers from among the circumcised who had come with Peter were amazed, because the gift of the Holy Spirit was poured out even on the Gentiles. For they were hearing them speaking in tongues and extolling God. Then Peter declared, "Can anyone withhold water for baptizing these people, who have received the Holy Spirit just as we have?" And he commanded them to be baptized in the name of Jesus Christ. Then they asked him to remain for some days. Act 10:44-48

In some instances, people were baptized in water and then they received the baptism of the Holy Spirit. In this instance, what happened to indicate that these people should also be baptized in water?

What does this indicate about the relationship between water baptism and baptism in the Holy Spirit in the New Testament church?

One who heard us was a woman named Lydia, from the city of Thyatira, a seller of purple goods, who was a worshiper of God. The Lord opened her heart to pay attention to what was said by Paul. And after she was baptized, and her household as well… Act 16:14-15

If Lydia was baptized after the Lord opened hear heart to pay attention to Paul, what does this tell us about the place of baptism in the way that Paul proclaimed the gospel?

And he said, "Into what then were you baptized?" They said, "Into John's baptism." And Paul said, "John baptized with the baptism of repentance, telling the people to believe in the one who was to come after him, that is, Jesus." On hearing this, they were baptized in the name of the Lord Jesus. And when Paul had laid his hands on them, the Holy Spirit came on them, and they began speaking in tongues and prophesying. Act 19:3-6

When we are water baptized, whose Name are we immersed into?

What connection between conversion, baptism in water, and baptism of the Holy Spirit do you observe?

God's patience waited in the days of Noah, while the ark was being prepared, in which a few, that is, eight persons, were brought safely through water. Baptism, which corresponds to this, now saves you, not as a removal of dirt from the body but as an appeal to God for a good conscience, through the resurrection of Jesus Christ…1 Pet.3:21-22

What is the relationship between baptism in water and saving faith?

Do you not know that all of us who have been baptized into Christ Jesus were baptized into his death? We were buried therefore with him by baptism into death, in order that, just as Christ was raised from the dead by the glory of the Father, we too might walk in newness of life. Rom. 6:3-4

When someone hears the gospel, how does baptism in water demonstrate their union with Jesus Christ?

According to what we've seen in the New Testament, answer the following as TRUE or FALSE?

_____ 1. Baptism can only be performed by ordained clergy

_____ 2. Baptism is sprinkling babies wearing pretty white dresses so they won't go to hell if they die at a young age.

_____ 3. Baptism should be delayed until converts have completed a "new believer's class" and give evidence of true conversion.

_____ 4. When someone believed the gospel, instead of being invited to pray a prayer of salvation with every eye closed and every head bowed, people were exhorted to repent and be baptized- to act on their faith and demonstrate the Kingdom of God by their obedience.

_____ 5. If you were baptized, this is a guarantee that you are saved.

_____ 6. We shouldn't talk about Jesus' command to repent and be baptized as we proclaim the gospel so that people will be sure to understand we are saved by grace.

KEY TAKE AWAYS:
   • Baptism is an act of faith and obedience for believers to fully identify themselves as disciple of Jesus Christ.

   • You can baptize anyone you lead to faith in Jesus Christ.

   • Baptism in itself doesn't save. Faith in Jesus Christ saves us. However, when baptism is given its proper place in the proclamation of the gospel, those who receive Jesus Christ as Lord act on their faith by baptism.

SUMMARY: Jesus Christ saves us by grace through faith apart from any works we do… including baptism. But Jesus and the apostles taught clearly that genuine faith in Jesus Christ brings us to recognize Him as Lord and act on the authority of God's Word to manifest the Kingdom. True saving faith acts on the authority of God's Word. Baptism brings our body and soul into union with Jesus Christ as we are immersed into His Name. The gospel makes our lives living demonstrations of the presence of the Kingdom of God through union with Jesus Christ. This begins with baptism into the Name of Jesus Christ as we are baptized in water.

III. LOOK OUT:
PRACTICE

1. Group Discussion

Here's the scenario: You just led your neighbor to saving faith in Jesus Christ. When you asked them if they were ready to be baptized they responded, "Oh I was baptized when I was a baby."

What are some things you might say to help them understand what baptism is and why it's important?

2. Role Play- Break into groups of 2 or 3. Take turns responding to your newly converted neighbor according to the scenario above. Rotate roles until each one has had the opportunity to respond.

- Give and receive feedback. What was good? What could make it better?
- Repeat the exercise incorporating the feedback you received.

PLAN

1. Find out if there is anyone in the group who has not been baptized since coming to faith in Jesus Christ. Make plans for their baptism.

2. Who can you teach what you just learned about baptism? Think about your family, friends, and acquaintances. Write their name(s) below and make plan to get together with them to share what you learned.

(Don't worry about whether people have been baptized or not. Just consider this an opportunity to practice sharing what you are learning to strengthen the faith of someone else)

3. If you know anyone who believes in Jesus but has not yet been baptized since becoming a believer, consider making an appointment with them to talk about their faith in Christ and the significance of baptism.

4. God wants to use you to multiply disciples who walk in supernatural power. Who can you take through the Immersed into God Interactive Training Manual? Ask God to give you one or two people to disciple for His glory. Is there anyone in your current group that might partner with you to start a new group together? The best way to learn is to teach others

PRAY

a. Pray for laborers to be sent out into the Harvest.

b. If anyone needs healing or prayer, lay hands and minister to one another.

APPENDIX 1
SUGGESTIONS FOR IMMERSED INTO GOD
GROUP LEADERS

1) Start NEW GROUPS from DAY 1- Here's how— Encourage each person in your group to begin to share with other people about the things that God is doing in their lives. As they find people who are interested and eager to grow, they should NOT invite them to join this group. Your group can receive visitors, but if someone wants to join, your group is CLOSED. Instead, challenge everyone in your group to begin to work through this same material with their friends and start a new groups!

2) Break the "Bible Study" Mold by doing the Word together- Your biggest job is to help people do what they dream of doing by:
- providing a supportive, encouraging, and focused environment
- celebrate people taking risks and overcoming their fears. Results will follow.
- do your assignments with people, especially the ones who need more support.
- keep everyone focused on Jesus and allowing Him to be Himself in us

3) Facilitate the meetings by being a Leader, a Coach, and a Learner. Use the manual as a tool to bring focus. Don't be the teacher or preacher. If you make your living room a mini-pulpit, your couch will become a comfy pew. These meetings are intended to draw out participation, involvement, and interaction..

4) Use the Training Manual as the playing field. When the "ball rolls out of bounds", refer to the manual to get things back on track. How? Usually a smile, a little chuckle, and an "Okay, now where were we? Let's get back on track gang" will do the trick.

5) During "Look Back":
- Start with a good example so people have an idea about how to share.
- If anyone is talking too much, just say, "This is good, but we need to wrap this up to allow time for others. 1 more minute."

6) Involve everyone during the LESSON by going around the room to take turns reading, calling out underlined phrases, circled phrases, answer to questions, etc.

7) Most topics will require more than one session, but be sure to divide every meeting evenly into three sections—"Look Back" "Lesson" and "Look Out"— so that every meeting contains encouragement and sharing, Bible learning, and practical hands-on ministry with goal setting for practical steps of faith.

8) Keep the focus on Jesus Christ and advancing His Kingdom because of His redeeming love. People are very prone towards falling into a "performance" mindset— basing their joy, security, and worth in their own ability to perform. Your main role is to help everyone keep their eyes on Jesus Christ. He's the only performer in the group! People are also very conditioned to maintain the status quo. The life of Jesus Christ must become our new normal, so we must declare war on the comfort zones of the flesh. It's not about us. It's about Jesus Christ and His love for others. Lead the way by example!

9) Take advantage of the additional resources to prepare yourself and encourage the group. I would highly recommend that you read the chapter of the book, *Immersed into God,* that corresponds with each lesson. Additionally, even if you decide not to watch the supplemental training videos as a group, it would be a very good idea for you to review these videos prior to each lesson. All these additional resources are available at FullSpeedImpact.com.

10) Multiply leaders for the group by selecting at least one or two apprentices from DAY 1. Give them additional responsibility, opportunities, and support. If you only have one or two people in your group, you should consider them both apprentices and give them opportunities to lead the group sessions while you are together so they develop their own leadership skills in a supportive environment.

APPENDIX 2
WHAT IF I DON'T FEEL "LED BY THE SPIRIT?"

As you grow into the image of Jesus Christ, you are going to take new steps of faith. Moving out of your comfort zone can be uncomfortable, but it's the good kind of "discomfort", like starting to use your muscles for exercising instead of just flipping the TV channels and opening new bags of potato chips. Every born again believer has the desire and the power to obey Jesus, but sometimes they mistake the uneasiness that arises from their own fears and the self-protective nature of the flesh for "not being led by the Spirit." One of the tactics of the enemy to keep God's people weak, fearful, and undisciplined is to cause us to misinterpret our personal discomfort as we begin to take new steps of faith and obedience as "not feeling led by the Holy Spirit."

Being led by the Spirit is simply following Jesus Christ, but now He lives inside you. Jesus tells everyone one of us, "If anyone would come after me, let him deny himself and take up his cross daily and follow me."(Luke9:23) Carrying a cross isn't necessarily comfortable, but it's the only way to follow Jesus. That's why Jesus died to give us the Comforter, the Holy Spirit. We never carry our cross alone or by our own power.

What does it mean to be "led by the Spirit?" Is it true that believers must receive a special nudge from the Holy Spirit before they can do what God's Word says we can do? Or must we have a specific prompting of the Lord before we can speak to someone about Jesus or lay hands on a sick person or make plans to undertake a specific step of faith to advance the Kingdom of God? Or can we just do what God says we can do in faith that He is always with us? Can we step out on the authority of God's Word with no special prompting from the Holy Spirit, and still count on the empowering of God?

It may come to your surprise to learn that the phrase "led by the Holy Spirit" is used only three times in the New Testament. Let's examine them one by one to see what we can learn. As we do so, we will be able to walk in confidence as we step out of our comfort zone.

1) Jesus was led by the Holy Spirit to fulfill a specific assignment for a season of solitude and fasting to overcome the temptations of devil. During this assignment, Jesus obeyed the written Word of God without any specific leading or prompting of the Spirit.

Then Jesus was led up by the Spirit into the wilderness to be tempted by the devil. And after fasting forty days and forty nights, he was hungry. And the tempter came and said to him, "If you are the Son of God, command these stones to become loaves of bread." But he answered, "It is written, "'Man shall not live by bread alone, but by every word that comes from the mouth of God.'" Mat 4:1-4

We see that the Spirit of God can give us specific direction about assignments from God on our life. However, we also see that we should follow Jesus' example, and do what God says to do in His Word, even in the absence of any special leading or prompting from the Spirit of God.

2) The Spirit of God guides us into personal understanding of all the truth in Christ, but we are responsible for walking in the truth once we understand it.

*I still have many things to say to you, but you cannot bear them now. When the Spirit of truth comes, **he will guide you into all the truth**, for he will not speak on his own authority, but whatever he hears he will speak, and he will declare to you the things that are to come. He will glorify me, for he will take what is mine and declare it to you.* John16:12-14

3) Sons of God, those who are born again, are always being led by the Spirit of God to put to death the misdeeds of the flesh by walking in confidence in our Father in heaven as we enjoy His fellowship.

*So then, brothers, we are debtors, not to the flesh, to live according to the flesh. For if you live according to the flesh you will die, but if by the Spirit you put to death the deeds of the body, you will live. For **all who are led by the Spirit of God are sons of God**. For you did not receive the spirit of slavery to fall back into fear, but you have received the Spirit of adoption as sons, by whom we cry, "Abba! Father!"* Rom 8:11-15

The Spirit of God leads us from the inside continuously to walk in our true identity as sons of God, just like Jesus Christ. He leads us to stop walking in bondage to sin, fear and insecurity — this would include putting to death fears that arise that attempt to keep us from walking like a son of God to set the captives free as we are growing into the image of Jesus Christ.

The Holy Spirit can (and does) give us specific direction and assignments (such as fasting for a season, for example.) When we receive a specific assignment from God, we do it. However, we don't *need* a specific assignment from God to do what He's already told us to do in His Word. We don't need to be led by the Spirit to walk in holiness or advance the Kingdom of God. We have a standing order to love God, love our neighbor as our self, and set the captives free. We don't need to worry "is this me, or is this God?" God has empowered us to walk in the authority of Jesus' words in the confidence that He is with us! The Spirit of God is constantly leading us to walk as Sons of God who are constantly walking in truth and being "doers of the Word."

Although we act on the special leadings of the Holy Spirit when God gives them, we don't require a special leading to walk by faith and to do what God has shown us in the Word. Believers who require a special prompting to step out in faith are actually disobeying the Word of God that tells us, *"**Be not** like a horse or a mule, without understanding, which must be curbed with bit and bridle, or it will not stay near you." (Psalm 32:9)* God wants us to walk like His children, not like a bunch of dumb mules who need to poked, prodded, and pulled to do what He's already shown and told us in His Word. Instead, He says, *"I will **instruct you and teach you in** the way you should go; I will **counsel you** with my eye upon you."* (Psalm 32:8) God wants us to learn from His Word and put it into practice in the confidence that He is always with us.

We see a perfect example of this in the book of Acts and the life of the Apostle Paul.

And they (the apostle Paul and his co-workers) *went through the region of Phrygia and Galatia, having been **forbidden by the Holy Spirit to speak the word in Asia**. And when they had come up to Mysia, they attempted to go into Bithynia, **but the Spirit of Jesus did not allow them**. So, passing by Mysia, they went down to Troas. And a vision appeared to Paul in the night: a man of Macedonia was standing there, urging him and saying, "Come over to Macedonia and help us." And when Paul had seen the vision, immediately we sought to go on into Macedonia, concluding that God had called us to preach the gospel to them.* Act 16:6-10

Apparently Paul was taking his entire team to Asia to preach the gospel without any specific leading from God. Otherwise the Holy Spirit would not have needed to intervene and tell Paul not to go to Asia at that time. When this happened, Paul didn't sit around waiting to be told where to go next. Paul continued to move based on the commission of Jesus Christ "Go into all the world and preach the gospel!" The next day, Paul just started off to preach the gospel "anywhere but Asia" and ended up going toward Bithynia. The Holy Spirit intervened with another specific leading, "No, not here. Not right now." God had a different assignment for Paul. That night, the Holy Spirit gave Paul a vision that sent him off to Macedonia along with his team.

What does it mean to be led by the Holy Spirit? It means that we are free to walk like sons and daughters of God and carry out the Word of God. It means that God is always working within us to lead us to walk like Jesus in freedom from sin and shame. The Holy Spirit is our Helper *as we step out in faith*. We don't walk around like slaves, afraid to take initiative. We are sons and daughters of the living God authorized to act as His ambassadors. We can always do what God says we can do, because He has said, "I am with you always." If we need specific direction, the Holy Spirit will give it to us, and we will act on it. Meanwhile, we are free to act on God's Word in the confidence that God is with us.

ADDITIONAL RESOURCES

Additional resources from Andy Hayner are available at **FullSpeedImpact.com**

IMMERSED INTO GOD (BOOK)

If you are ready for a life filled with God's love and power that impacts the world around you, *Immersed into God* will give you the Biblical and practical understanding you need. It's over You will learn to:

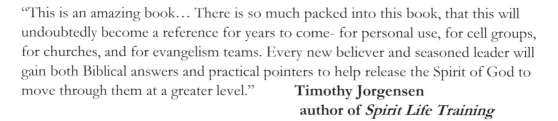

➢ Establish Your identity in Christ

➢ Heal the sick like Jesus

➢ Discern demonic oppression and set people free

➢ Minister in the power of the Holy Spirit

➢ Become a supernatural disciple-maker capable of reaching the unchurched

➢ Enjoy God's presence in your daily activities

➢ Demonstrate the presence of the Kingdom of God wherever you go

➢ And much more!

"This is an amazing book… There is so much packed into this book, that this will undoubtedly become a reference for years to come- for personal use, for cell groups, for churches, and for evangelism teams. Every new believer and seasoned leader will gain both Biblical answers and practical pointers to help release the Spirit of God to move through them at a greater level."   **Timothy Jorgensen**
author of *Spirit Life Training*

SPIRIT CRY- Declarations of a Child of God in the Embrace of the Father!

Activate your spirit by using the Scriptures to hear and speak from the Spirit of the Son of God within you. You'll learn to:

➢ *Experience* Your Identity in Christ in personal fellowship with God

➢ Break free from self-condemnation, fear, and insecurity

➢ See the revelation of Jesus Christ in the Scriptures and inside of you with penetrating insight

➢ Transform your mindsets for a supernatural lifestyle

ABOUT THE AUTHOR

Andy Hayner mobilizes believers to walk in fullness of Jesus Christ world-wide. He is recognized for having a gift to impart a profound revelation of the believer's union with Jesus Christ in a simple, understandable way that unleashes greater depths of the love and power of God. He has a passion for hands-on disciple making that has been developed through over twenty years of Christian service as a missionary, a pastor, and a church planter. He is the founder of Full Speed Impact Ministries and volunteers as a Regional Director for John G. Lake Ministries, the oldest and most successful healing ministry in existence today. He holds a Masters of Divinity from Columbia International University Graduate School of Missions. He resides in Wisconsin with his wife and three children.

A missionary at heart, Andy travels widely to ministers to churches, small groups, conferences, and individuals wherever God opens the door. Although he travels widely, he endeavors to establish ongoing relationships with churches to be a regular outside resource for the sake of the Kingdom. To enquire about having Andy minister in your area, please contact Andy directly at FullSpeedAndy@gmail.com.

20476607R00078

Made in the USA
Middletown, DE
30 May 2015